Dancing with God

Moving Into Your Destiny

Briget Carlson

"You have turned my mourning into joyful dancing. You have taken away my clothes of mourning and clothed me with joy."

Psalm 30:11

Contents

Acknowledgement

Eric, you are the love of my life. As my husband, your ability to see beyond my short comings and help me to achieve what God has called me to do is priceless. There are no words I can say that would adequately describe how valuable and incredible you are to me. Thank you for all your help with rewriting, editing and giving me time and space to grow.

Joshua and Kelly Carlson, you are my precious gifts from God. You gave me a reason to live when I wanted to give up. Joshua and Kelly, your knowledge and support with computers during this writing process, was extremely helpful. Thank you, Angel and "J".

Courtney Talley, know that even though you are all grown up and don't live at home anymore you are still a very important part of this story. Thank you for always believing in my dreams. You will never know how much your compassion and words of encouragement inspired me. Thank you Princess.

Dad , thank you for just being you. You have always been my anchor and someone I could depend on in case of emergencies. I am blessed to have a dad like you.

Pastor Dave and Dolores Meyer, your faithfulness and dedication to the Lord has changed my life forever. Your steadfastness and and love for the truth has helped me to receive and proclaim the Word of God as it is written. You two will always have a special place in my heart.

Amy Lynn Maxwell, you are a trusted friend. I miss our Tuesday night bible study over the phone as well as our prayer time. Thank you for believing in my dream and praying with me through to it's completion.

i

Leah Chapman, my first editor, I was nervous to release this book and allow someone to know my deepest thoughts. I thank God that He put you in my life to be the first person outside of my family to read it. Your words of encouragement and dedication for excellence has brought this book to a higher level of clarity. You are a precious jewel.

Tony Llewllyn , my final editor, you are a genius at those finishing touches. Thank you for making me look good.

Living Word Prayer group, thank you for all you prayers. I am proud you are my church family and I love you all.

Kris Newman, my Facebook friend. You pointed me in the right direction and gave me wisdom to navigate through the publishing stage. Your words of encouragement pushed me passed this unknown territory and help me to believe this book could be accomplished. It is good to have friends that have paved the way.

Jesus, I saved the best for last. When You entered my life that one desperate afternoon and showed me that You loved me, my life has changed forever. Anything that is good or praise worthy in me is Your handwork in my life. You continually amaze me with Your endless mercies, so that through me, others can see You. My life is Yours. You have captured my heart and as your dance partner I will go wherever You lead me.

Forward

Have you ever had a dream that you wanted so bad that you would be willing to give up everything just to obtain it? A longing so deep that you would push aside any doubts or fears just to receive it? My dream and I believe it's the dream that God has put in everyone of us before we were born, it is to be loved unconditional by our creator and to know the purpose for our life.

My story begins in how God patiently waited for me to give Him my broken heart so that He could heal it. It is a love story about an extraordinary merciful God who came down to rescue me out of a prison of darkness and despair and give me life. I believe God created us for a purpose and He is waiting for us to surrender ourselves to Him so He can put His dream (dance) within us.

My hope is that you will see through these pages a powerful, compassionate and amazing God who can turn any situation around and bring healing and restoration. A God who looks past our sins and brokenness and see who we were meant to be. If you think your life is beyond repair or God couldn't change the mess that you are in. Let me encourage you today, for the bible says, "that nothing is impossible for Him" (God). (Luke 1:37) Did you hear that, He can fix everything. That's good news!

Do you want to step into a life of healing, restoration and abundance? Come along with me and experience the power of the Holy Spirit and the life giving Word as you receive the truth as it is written in the Bible. If God could take a depressed, suicidal mother of three from the pit of hell and turn her life around, imagine what He could do for you?

If you will stay with me through this whole journey I promise you that you will find the key to eternal life. You will not have to wonder if you are saved or if God really loves you. The security of knowing the truth through the Word and experiencing the power of the Holy Spirit will transform you so that you are able to have a more intimate relationship with God.

If you are reading this book right now, I believe its God ordained. He is extending His hand to you and asking you, "will you dance with me?" My prayer is that you will say, yes" for He is the greatest dance partner the world has ever seen and He will lovingly teach you every step of the way.

You don't need to fear the future or wonder if you can achieve what He is calling you to do. For it says in the bible, "He would never leave you or forsake you. (Hebrews 13:5) That's right, He has never given up on you. He's wanting and ready to help you no matter where you are in life. When you accept His love He draws close to you so that he can personally lead you to your destiny.

There is no greater joy then experiencing the unconditionally love of God moving through you by the power of Holy Spirit as you surrender your heart to Him. This book will lead you into the arms of your Father who is eagerly waiting to show you His love and blessings. You have nothing to lose by reading this little book (but maybe a little time) but if you believe and receive the "Word of God" it will change you into the person you were meant to be. If God can do it for me He can do it for you.

God bless,

Briget Carlson
One of Jesus dance partner's

Chapter One

My Broken Dream

"Is there no medicine in Gilead? Is there no physician there? Why is there no healing for the wounds of my people?" Jeremiah 8:22

I was born in July of 1964, to Peter and Shelia Lauder in West Allis, Wisconsin. I was the oldest child from a typical Midwest, middle-class family. I was confident, inquisitive, and loved to learn new things. My father worked in banking, while my mother worked part-time as a nurse, raising 3 children. Dad was a family man, who loved to spend time with his kids. Whenever Dad would go somewhere, he would always take one of us with him. Of course being the oldest, I had the benefit of going places with him the most. Dad really enjoyed teaching us all kinds of things. He taught me how to golf, fish, drive a boat, change a tire, and the list goes on. Besides teaching us how to have fun, he showed us how to be honorable and respectful of others. We were his pride and joy, and he couldn't wait to show us the world through his eyes.

My Dad took me under his wing, and encouraged me that whatever I put my mind to, I could do. Because he showed faith in me, I desired to make him proud. My Dad had an adventurous heart, and a burden to fulfill his dreams. His example taught me to always dream big and believe in the impossible. I thought the world of my dad: There was no one greater, smarter, or stronger than him. I loved and trusted him with all my heart, and I always knew that I was safe in his arms.

When I was 6, we moved from West Allis to a new home in Waukesha, Wisconsin. The neighborhood provided exciting, youthful adventures and new friends. Life was awesome and then it happened … my younger sister, Colleen Patricia, or "CP" as we called her, was diagnosed with a brain tumor. Life would change dramatically. The bright skies of childhood were suddenly dimmed by clouds of uncertainty and despair.

One night at dinner, my mom noticed that CP was eating with her left hand, which was odd because she was right-handed. When mom asked her to eat with her right hand, CP told her that she couldn't. Mom asked me if I knew why she couldn't use her right hand. The only thing I told her was that a few days prior, CP had asked me to button her shirt. I just figured she was being lazy, but being the older sister, I knew it was the right thing to do to help her. I didn't think much of it at the time. Mom immediately called her friend, Carol, who was a fellow nurse and asked her for her opinion. They both agreed that CP needed to be taken to the Emergency Room and examined immediately.

While my brother and I were sitting in the waiting room of the ER, I saw my mom leaning heavily on my dad and crying uncontrollably. A deep pit grew in my stomach as I knew something was seriously wrong. That night, CP was checked into the hospital. While my Dad drove my brother and I home, I asked him what was wrong with her. Not wanting us to worry, my father simply told us that they found something on her brain that was making her sick. Instantly I thought *how can her brain be sick? Did she put something in it to make herself sick? No, she was always the one in the family who was kind and so forgiving.* Whenever I asked her not to tell our parents I lied to them or hurt her, she'd keep it a secret for me. That's when the thought hit me: *You made her sick because you made her keep secrets from our parents.* I instantly felt conviction that somehow CP's cancer was all my fault.

As soon as we returned home, I knelt down beside my bed and began to pray to God. I asked Him to forgive me for making her keep secrets from our parents and not being a good sister. I pleaded with Him to heal her and needed to know I was forgiven. I promised I would be good sister and obedient to my parents from that moment forward.

For the next year and half, I rarely saw my mom and dad. CP spent more time at the hospital than at home. Truly the cancer began to dictate the schedules of our lives. My mom would spend most nights by CP's side. Sometimes, what we forgot is that CP was a kid and she wasn't sure what was going on and needed her mom and dad's love and assurance. Since Dad worked days, he'd visit her at night. With both parents being gone so much, my brother and I spent many days at our relatives' homes, and during the summer, at our neighbor's. I stayed strong, praying and trying to be good so that God would answer my prayer, and put my family back together. I prayed because I knew that God was good, and that He wouldn't allow someone so young to die. Right?

A year and half has passed and I remember my mom coming to pick up my brother and I from the neighbor's house, where we spent most of the summer. This was odd because normally my dad would pick us up after work and take us home to make us dinner. I was so happy to see my mom, and I knew there was unexpected news. Mom went inside to talk to the neighbor and I opened the passenger door of the car and got in. Suddenly, I turned to see two of CP's favorite dolls sitting in the backseat. Why would CP's dolls be in the car and not with her? I turned and gazed toward the house and thought *is it possible that CP died?* I immediately pushed that thought aside. God wouldn't let her die. She was only seven years old. God can do anything. In Sunday School, I remember learning all the miracles God performed in the Bible. God loved CP; He wouldn't let anything happen to her. I'd been praying every day; surely God heard me. As much as I didn't want to ask, I did. When mom got in the car, I asked her, "Why are CP's dolls in the car?" She turned to me with tears in her eyes and said, "Your sister passed away this morning." There I was, eight years old, and my entire world began to crumble. I was in complete shock. I stared out the window, holding back the tears, wondering why my prayers had gone unheard.

This was my first experience with grief, and I found it to be very heavy and overwhelming. I believe that grief has the same effect on a person regardless of the age; it doesn't matter whether you're 8 or 80 years old.

I have heard it said that the first stage of grief is denial. Although I went to the funeral not fully believing that I was about to bury my sister, she was dead. It was hard to tell how my dad was taking things because he showed no emotion. I, in turn, did my best not to show any emotion either; however, on the inside, I was broken. Everything inside of me was crying and begging for God to bring her back to life. CP and I were eleven months apart, and we shared everything. I couldn't recall a time in my young life that she wasn't a part of. Although we were total opposites in our looks, personality, and demeanor, we went together like peanut butter and jelly, and our lives were so intertwined that I didn't know how to live without her. Every night before I went to bed, I would ask God, "Please bring CP home tonight so that I can say good-bye to her and tell her how much that I love her." And yet, like a thief in the night, she was taken from me before I could say good-bye to her.

As in any grieving process, denial can soon turn into guilt if the relationship ended without reconciliation. I began to think back on how I'd taken CP for granted. I would push her aside while knowing that she'd always be there if I needed a friend. My guilt turned into remorse. Now I would give anything to tell her how much I cared for her or how much I appreciated who she was. I just wanted a second chance to make things right with her, but the opportunity was gone, and the wound it left was deep and raw. Each night, I would cry myself to sleep because my heart was shattered into a million pieces, and I didn't know how to put it back together again.

One night, my mother came downstairs because she had heard me crying, and when she was tried to comfort me, I asked her," Why doesn't dad ever cry? Doesn't he love CP?" My mom told me that he was trying to stay strong for us, and she confessed to me that some nights, she would hear him crying in his sleep. My dad had lost his little girl, and he was trying to stay strong for us. I think that I finally realized that my dad was broken too, and because of that, he was never going to be able to give me the comfort and security that I so desperately wanted or needed. The man that I knew who could solve anything and take any situation and make it ok ... was broken.

If Dad wasn't going to be able to fix everything, I had to figure out a way to insulate myself from pain. It was at this point that I took matters into my own hands. The way I began to deal with pain and grief was to bury it; put it somewhere in which I didn't have to feel or look at. I'd bury it so deep and then wrap it with something solid and unbreakable. This was the point where my heart began to harden.

As if losing my sister to cancer wasn't bad enough, within a span of three months, my best friend moved away, and my dog died. I just couldn't get any relief from the pain inside, and when I went to school, there wasn't a single classmate that would talk to me because they didn't know what to say or how to comfort me. My friends stopped coming by the house, and I felt utterly alone. My anger began to grow within me, and I felt trapped in this cocoon of grief that I felt unable to escape. I didn't know what to do with the frustration and anger that was growing inside me.

Everyday, I would try to run from the pain, but it would eventually catch up with me. I continued to pray to God and ask Him to let me see my sister again, as I believed that this would heal me. However, I remember another voice that entered into my mind, a voice that said: *God doesn't care about you. People will always hurt you by leaving you. Your sister left, your dad left, your friends left, and even your dog left now.* The voice was so real and convincing that I received it and turned a new corner; one that would lead down a very dark path. I told myself that I couldn't take the grief anymore. I drew a line in the sand with God, angrily telling Him, "I don't believe in your power anymore, and it looks like Satan has won," and to top that off, "I will not love people with all of my heart because they are weak and eventually leave you when times get tough." Those kinds of words take on a life of their own. At that moment, I somehow knew that I turned my heart away from God, and with that, began my journey to hell.

Chapter Two

A Dream Dies

"There is a path before each person that seems right, but it ends in death." Proverbs 14:12

What is hell? It has been described as a very dark, empty place without God. This hell I lived in made me feel such an overwhelming pain and self-loathing that I started searching for harmful things I thought would make me feel better. By the age of fifteen, I began to smoke cigarettes, drink alcohol and even dabble in drugs. This seemed to help alleviate some of the pain inside me, but it was only temporary and left me wanting more. As I entered into puberty and was becoming a young woman, guys began to show me attention. Somewhere within this mess of emotion, I still felt that there was a glimmer of hope that I could be loved and my heart put back together. I hoped beyond hope there was someone out there who could love and heal my brokenness even though I felt so unworthy of any type of love. With that being said, I began the search for that perfect person who'd never leave me, of whom I could trust and feel safe with.

Once I started dating, I was picky with whom I would or wouldn't allow into my heart. Every guy went through a battery of tests before I would even consider him dating material. If they passed my so-called test, I would let my heart open a little, but it was minimal because it wasn't worth the pain if they walked away. When a guy would hurt me, there weren't any second chances. My heart had hardened so much by this time that it never developed past an 8-year-old child who swore she would never love again. If emotional pain came my direction, I redirected it to an old target: Me. I felt that someone needed to take the blame for all of this hurt, and so I began to punish myself by not allowing anyone to love me.

As a young woman, I had truly become my own god because I knew what was best for me, and I could take care of myself. I had learned to protect myself from pain so well that I barely ever felt any other emotions. As you can see, this way of thinking is not very conducive to having a long-term relationship with anyone. So my social circles became smaller, which ended up causing me to feel very isolated and scared.

When I was nineteen years old, I started dating a man named Eric Carlson. I had dated a few guys, but Eric was different. Those old feelings were still there. The minute I began to entertain any type of positive feelings, I'd push him away. But no matter how many times I pushed him away, he would always come back and try to work things out. I think he understood in some way how I felt deep inside. Eric was so patient and understanding. He had the ability to communicate his feelings and helped me to understand and accept that I could be forgiven. We dated for two and half years until Eric asked me to marry him.

Although I knew he wasn't perfect, there was something about him that gave me hope, and I started to believe that love really existed. I did my best to be a good wife and make him happy, and after two years into our marriage, we decided to have children.

Eric had his own baggage that he was dealing with for years: He didn't like himself very much and wasn't happy with where he was in life. The way he avoided the pain was alcohol and drugs. We were an interesting couple to say the least. I thought children would bring about a sense of responsibility, but that didn't happen. The extra responsibility of having a family seemed to make Eric all the more reclusive. It was about this time in our marriage that Eric really began to abuse alcohol and misuse our finances.

I wanted to end my marriage, but I remembered my mom's stern statement before I got married, and it seemed to echo in my mind: "Once you're married, don't ever think you're coming back home if it doesn't work."

This might sound harsh, but I thank God that she told me that because those words kept me from giving up on our marriage.

As we continued to have our struggles, the pain and the problems of our marriage started to overwhelm me, and the old feelings of grief returned. I decided to go back to school because I thought that if my marriage didn't work out, I would at least be able to take care of myself and our children. Eric's drinking got worse: I'd find bottle after bottle of hard liquor hidden around the apartment. Here was the man that I thought I could count on for any problem and he would make it ok, but once again, another broken man, just like my dad.

In the fall of 1991, his family did an intervention. Eric's drinking was out of control. That evening turned out to be a godsend. It was a tough night, but Eric promised me he'd give AA a try. January 1, 1992, Eric had his last drink. After a few months, it seemed as though the peace was coming back into the marriage. My desire to finish school vanished as we moved forward with our life. Eric started taking control of his life and decided to go back to school. Having a degree was something his father always wanted for him. Eric was set and determined to make it happen. Unfortunately, it came at the   expense of myself and our children.

We soon moved into our first home. Our children were four and two at the time, and like any young mother, there were times when I felt overwhelmed. Eric was working so hard, trying to make ends meet. He'd work a 10-12 hour day, go to class at night, and then homework every weekend. That didn't leave much time for me and the kids. With Eric being gone most of the time, I became the one in charge, so I tried my best to raise the children with good values.

Life became challenging for me because as our son grew, he wanted to fight my authority twenty-four-seven. My emotional state was wearing me down because I never expected one of my children to be so strong-willed. I'd tell Eric my concerns, but he was so wrapped up in work and college, it felt like he never heard me. I felt all alone. My vision of marriage, one man and one woman, "working together" to raise healthy children that are emotionally and physically well was discarded because it seemed like I was doing this on my own.

Once again, I felt alone and became depressed. I was married to a man who was trying to do the best for his family and tried so hard to provide for us. I literally had the American dream. Why did I still feel so empty inside? I just couldn't shake this feeling, no matter how much energy I put into this family. I was depressed.

I would describe depression as a cycle where you are

in the middle of the ocean, and you have no life preserver. It feels as if you are dog paddling and looking everywhere for land, and then all of the sudden, out of nowhere, a big wave hits you, and it takes you under. The wave that I'm speaking of is when you think you have disappointed someone you love, and the spirit of failure tries to pull you down under the water. Your mind begins to race, trying to figure out how you can escape this pain, but your heart doesn't find any way out. This is what I call depression. This emotion will pull a person down until you cry out for help, or cause depression so deep within you that when you think of death, it seems like the only solution to your problem.

Between raising children and all the challenges that went with it, I started to feel overwhelmed and there were days that I just wanted to walk away and give it all up. I told Eric how I felt. I needed a release, a way out of this cycle, some place I could clear my mind and find some peace. Then the most amazing thing happened ... I found myself sitting in a church.

Chapter Three

A New Hope

"Be still, and know that I am God!" Psalm 46:10

There was a Catholic Church near our house, and I began to attend Saturday evening services. Quite honestly, I used it primarily as an outlet to get out of the house and have some solitude as opposed to taking any real spiritual or religious significance out of it. I would sit there during service, taking in the words and music, and tears would begin to well up in my eyes. What was wrong with me? I could never understand what was happening to me, but looking back now, I can see that God was reaching out to me with compassion, tugging at my heart strings, letting me know He never left and wanted to help me. All I needed to do was call out to Him.

One day, as I was watching a TV program, I started to feel as if there might be some hope for me. The speaker said that the sadness I felt could be solved but that I had to get to the root of the problem. By the end of the program, he encouraged the audience to sit still before

God and connect with him by just waiting on Him. I was determined to get to the root of this depression so I turned the program off, believing there was hope for me. As I sat on the floor and closed my eyes, I said to God, "If you still love me, I need your help." I sat there, getting my mind and my heart to be as still as I could, and I experienced God. I could feel Him drawing me to Him with great urgency and love, and I knew that the life that I was living was a place that was so far from God, and yet I knew He loved me and wasn't mad at me. After that experience, I stood up and said to God, "I want to know you God, and I don't want anyone to teach me, but you." A thought then came to my mind that I should read the Bible, so as soon as Eric came home from work, I asked him, "Where did you put the Bible that your dad gave us last Christmas?" I couldn't wait to start reading it because I wanted to know God, and I knew that He was my only hope.

The next day, as I sat at my kitchen table and opened the Bible to the first page, I began to read. I'm not sure how long I read, but after I finished, I went to my bedroom, and I began to talk to Him about all my problems. When I felt that I had said everything that needed to be said, I sat there and waited for Him to respond. Because of the significance of this experience for me, I made it an everyday routine from that moment forward, and it transformed my life.

As I began this journey to know God, I began to imagine what plan He might have for me. I was determined to know who Jesus was, and I knew my only hope to know Him was by reading his Word. I wanted to know what God had to say. Given I'd never thought to read this book nor encouraged to til this period, I now know it was the Holy Spirit prompting me, and that this was not my idea but God's.

The next morning, as I prepared my breakfast of a bagel and a steaming cup of coffee, I set out to read in the first chapter and first verse in the Bible: *"In the beginning God created the heavens and the earth. The earth was empty, a formless mass cloaked in darkness. And the Spirit of God was hovering over its surface. Then God said, "Let there be light," and there was light." (Genesis 1:1-3 NLT)*

I thought to myself, "Am I doing this right?" However, that thought only stopped me for about a second because I was determined to know God for myself. I was on a mission, and I was determined to read the Bible each day. I would read one to two chapters until I was finished. This was my new goal, and nothing was going to stop me.

I had very little understanding about the stories in the

bible, but I did remember the story of Adam and Eve. As I read the first couple chapters about how God created the earth, I was amazed by His power and creativity. Before God even created man and woman, he had created the heavens and the earth, and it struck me how much attention and consideration he had put into creating a beautiful place for the human race. After I read the first two chapters, I was hooked. I didn't find the Bible boring; rather, I found it exciting and enlightening. In fact, I thought to myself, "Why hadn't I read this book before?" I didn't know it at the time, but God was opening a window to my heart so that I could see His glorious plan. He revealed to me that He wanted to reconcile my life back to Him, and every word gave me a new understanding of God's love for mankind and how He truly desired a relationship with His creation.

I was still hungry for more of God and wanted to experience His presence again, like I had on the living room floor. So after I had finished my breakfast, I marked my page and went into my bedroom. The only way I knew how to seek and experience Him was to open myself up and get quiet. As I sat on the floor, I began to quiet myself and pray, "God, I open up my heart and mind to you." I wanted to hear from God so badly, but my thoughts kept jumping all over the place, so I just kept repeating that same phrase, "God, I open up my heart and mind to you." It was certainly a simple prayer, but I discovered that as I kept repeating this phrase, my heart rate slowed down, followed by my mind, until my body came to a complete rest.

In the Bible, it says, *"Be still, and know that I am God: I will be exalted in the earth. The lord of hosts is with us; the God of Jacob is our refuge. Selah."* (Psalms *46:10 NLT).*

At the time, I didn't know that what I was doing was scriptural, but I believed that if I waited for God, He would come back and speak to me in the deepest part of my soul. I was so desperate to know what real love was, therefore I was willing to wait.

At about this time, I started to journal so that I could remember everything that God was revealing to me. My first entry in my journal was dated 10/10/1998. Here's what it read:

I see a white bag of money, with lots of cash in it. Its looks like one of those white linen cloth bags in an old western movie, and this bag of cash is just sitting on the floor. I also see a man laying on a hospital gurney, and it looks like he has been wounded. I imagine being held by God and telling Him how much I love Him, and I began to cry.

I wasn't crying because I was sad, but because I felt secure and loved. I had not felt these feelings in such a long time, and my heart was beginning to come alive with different emotions. The only recent emotions I felt were anger, frustration and bitterness. But now, I sensed that all that pain inside could go away.

What I find amazing in God is that my anger at Him never stopped Him from pursuing my heart: He didn't let my imperfection and my inability to communicate effectively stop Him from revealing His affection to me. Although I didn't even know what I needed from Him, He knew exactly what it was.

I wasn't quite sure how to share this news with anyone. Would they laugh, or possibly discourage me from continuing on this new journey? Could they even understand the love that I had found? So for now, I kept my journey to myself.

I can't begin to tell you how excited I was. Once again I was filled with hope, and I knew that if I connected with God, I would be healed and have my life back. Whatever was happening, whatever I was experiencing was so precious. I didn't want to let it go … I wouldn't let it go … I wanted more.

Chapter Four

Get Up and Dance

*"So be strong and courageous, all you who put your
hope in the Lord!" Psalm 31:24*

Hope is defined in the Webster's dictionary as: The
feeling that what is wanted can be had or that events will
turn out well. 2. To look forward to with desire and
reasonable confidence. 3. To believe or trust.1

There was a movie made about ten years ago called
"Hope Floats" with Sandra Bullock, who played Birdee
Pruitt. The movie is set in Chicago, where Connie,
Birdee's best friend, appears on a trashy daytime talk
show and tells a nationwide TV audience about her affair
with Birdee's husband. Connie's revelation leads to
public humiliation for Birdee.

Birdee and her young daughter, Bernice, move back to
Texas to live with her eccentric mother. Since most of
Smithville saw the TV show, embarrassment continues to
stalk Birdee. Her moment of glory as the homecoming
"Queen of Corn" has not been forgotten by handyman

Justin Matisse, the first guy who kissed her back in high school, so a romance soon begins.

The pivotal part of the movie is when Birdee's mom dies, then her husband, Bill, returns to Texas. After the funeral, he asks Birdee to sign the divorce papers. Their daughter, Bernice, is distraught and asks her father if she can come and live with him. He looks her in the eyes and tells her she must stay with her mom because he is starting a new life with Connie, his new girlfriend. Bernice won't accept it and throws her suitcase into his car and gets in. Her father takes her out of the car and tells her she needs to be strong and be good for her mom. Bernice begins to wail and plead with her dad to take her with him. He turns and gets back into his car and drives off, leaving Bernice running after the vehicle, yelling at the top of her lungs, "Daddy, come back"! There is a point where she stops running after the car but continues to become hysterical begging for her daddy to come back. Her hope for the future, as she knew it, had been destroyed by the one that she loved the most. Deep down in her heart, something broke, and if she was to survive, she would have to be willing to go down this new path with her mom, without her dad in her life.

Hope is a funny thing because just when you think there is nothing left to hope for, life changes and surprises you. Just like "Birdee" felt in the movie, there was a time in my life when I could relate to her feelings of overwhelming shame and humiliation. My shame, however, was not that my husband was having an affair with my best friend, but the shame of being an alcoholic.

From the age of seventeen on, I was labeled a "problem social drinker". My mom was constantly concerned that my binge drinking was leading me down a path of self-destruction. Just to appease her incessant pestering, I allowed her to take me to an office where I was to speak to a counselor and answer several questions about my drinking habits. At the end of our session, he came to the conclusion that I was a problem social drinker. The only difference, in my opinion, between an alcoholic and a problem social drinker, is how often you get drunk a week. Even though most alcoholic's drink everyday, I drank every weekend, with the goal of getting drunk until I passed out.

This lifestyle of drinking and partying continued on. I became pregnant with our first child at 25. I had nine months of sobriety and became the proud mother of a baby girl, then two years later, a son, and many years after that, another precious baby girl. My husband and I were a young couple with three children and one income, and we had little money to hire a babysitter and go out. Things had changed a bit now: Eric was a recovering alcoholic for six years and no longer drank. After a long week with three kids, when I had the opportunity, I was ready to party. I just needed to cut loose and be free from all of my responsibilities, especially the self-imposed standard of perfection as a wife and mother. Heavy drinking became a crutch because it had truly become for me, "liquid courage". It helped me step out of my comfort zone and allow "the true me" to come pouring out. It really didn't matter to me whether these feelings were good or bad; I just wanted to be either heard or noticed for who I was. The only problem was that I couldn't really tell you who I was as a person. I had lost my identity somewhere in our marriage. All I knew was that there was such an emptiness.

I felt as if I were a failure at my life. I didn't think that my husband needed me, and I was overwhelmed with the responsibility of caring for three children. Many times my kids would act out and as a new mom, I wasn't sure how to deal with all these behavioral issues. I actually started to believe that everything that was wrong with my children was somehow my fault. I refused to *reach out* for help because of pride and shame.

Depression is like a magnet: It attracts so many other unhealthy destructive feelings, such as insanity and suicide. In fact, my depression invited loneliness into my life. I never dreamt that being married and having children was going to be so overpowering. When we first got married, I had this dream that my husband and I would rear our children together, and that he would see how valuable I was to him. I dreamt that our children would respect and love me for all that I'd given up for them. This, however, was not how I imagined it would be, and somehow, the loneliness became a constant reminder that I was not valuable or worthy of love. I felt that if I could be successful as a mother and wife, I could receive the love that I so desperately wanted.

There was someone else in our marriage; this actor was not physical but abstract in design She was fighting hard to lure Eric's attention away from me. If I had to name her, I would call her "Fear of Failure"; to the outside world, they would call her "Success". My spirit was lonely, but I didn't know how to tell Eric that "she" was taking him away. Part of me was angry and frustrated because he just couldn't see that he was being manipulated by "her" charm of honor and respect from others. I didn't want to be a nagging wife and make him think that I didn't appreciate all the hard work that he was doing, but his priorities had changed. His desire to be successful had bumped us out of first place in his heart, and I didn't know how to win him back. Something had to give; I was going out of my mind.

I can recall a time when my husband and I went to a wedding, and of course, I began to drink heavily. The emotional walls began to come down, and I was quick to open up to anyone who would listen. I was starving for affection and the attention of a man to tell me I had value. I also enjoyed making my husband jealous because in my intoxicated mind, he did it to me everyday by ignoring me and the kids. I was angry at him because I felt that he was not keeping our marriage vow. *Didn't he promise that he would love and cherish me all the days of our lives?* In our marriage, I felt like a maid and a nanny, but definitely not a wife. For just a few hours, alcohol made me feel free to be me, powerful and important. I didn't care if it hurt my husband or family. I selfishly and irresponsibly made it about me, and when my husband wanted to leave the wedding that night, I became so irritated with him. Once we left, I had to go back to being the "maid and mother." I knew Eric was irritated as well because he was in his sixth year of sobriety and was getting tired of waiting for a wife he could be proud of. As I said, something had to give.

When we arrived home, Eric handed me the money to give to the babysitter, and told me to send her out to the car so that he could give her a ride home. As I was heading towards the front door, I stumbled back and forth. It was all I could do to try and appear relatively sober while talking to the babysitter. Looking back, I don't remember her leaving the house or if I'd even made any sense. I know I gave her the money because Eric asked her if I did when she got in the car. After she left, I headed to the bathroom. All that courage I drank was about to come up. I remember I threw up for hours, just clinging to the toilet bowl and wanting to die. Hangovers are wonderful things: They're little reminders that you had too much to drink and that there were probably some things you'd rather not remember. The next day's hangover was a constant reminder of shame and guilt. It hung on me as if it were a heavy coat that I couldn't take off on a warm summer day. My mind raced back in time, and I thought about all that I'd said and done the night before. I began the ritual of telling myself that I would never drink again as I'd done so many times before. For the first time, I didn't just embarrass Eric, but I embarrassed my oldest daughter, Courtney. We not only knew the babysitter but the babysitter's parents. What did the babysitter tell her parents? Did she tell them that I was a drunken mess and slurred my words as I attempted to thank her for watching Courtney? Had she left the house when I bolted for the toilet? Was she in the house as I got sick over and over? Was she wondering whether she could leave the kids with me while Eric took her home? Did she tell her parents all of this? I felt such disgust and shame.

The irony was that nine days prior, I had started reading the Word of God. I knew something was beginning to change in me, and the abuse of alcohol was starting to convict me. I was finally realizing that I was not only doing this to myself, but to my family as well. I knew that I was wrong and needed to change.

After that night, my Journal entry for 10/21/1998 said:

"I've asked God to forgive me many times for my behavior on Saturday night. I promised God and my husband that I would never drink again. I'm having a hard time forgiving myself. I want to be a friend of God's again."

It was decision time. Either it was drinking and escape… or God, and I guess I wasn't sure what to expect. If I chose God, I'd have to give up drinking forever.

I chose to give up drinking and God honored my prayer and took away my desire for alcohol that day. He is a merciful God and I want to give Him all the praise and glory for this miracle!

Chapter Five

Listening to the Music

"I pray that God, the source of hope, will fill you completely with joy and peace because you trust in him. Then you will overflow with confident hope through the power of the Holy Spirit." Romans 15:13

My passion for God began to grow even stronger, and I discovered Christian radio for the first time. I heard the "Good News" that Jesus was born of a woman, fully man and yet fully God. The Bible speaks about the kingdom of God and how Jesus performed so many healings and miracles. He had come to earth to die for our sins so that we could be forgiven. He would have to go through a horrible death on a cross; he was buried for three days but on the third day would rise again. It says in the Bible:

"For God loved the world so much that he gave his one and only Son, so that everyone who believes in him will not perish but have eternal life." (John 3:16 NLT)

I had never truly understood the love of God before this moment. My view of God had been that He was all-powerful and all-knowing. But, could He forgive me of all my sins and give me a new life in Him?

I want to share a vision that God gave me, shortly after I heard the "Good News" on the radio. A vision is when God reveals a deep, hidden, secret within the Word of God to a person through prayer, which cannot be perceived by the natural man. When you receive these visions through prayer, it will excite and fill your mind with wonder and admiring views of God. It says in the Bible:

"Open my eyes to see the wonderful truths in your instructions." (Psalm 119:18 NLT)

The vision begins with me curled up in the corner of a dirt cell, far beneath the earth. I know in my heart that I have no hope of ever getting out of this despairing place. I look around and there is no color or light in this room, until suddenly, I see a few other people in the same state that I am in, and I realize that I'm not alone in the cell.

I then notice a man standing next to me, and he

extends his right hand. Without saying a word, I instantly knew he wanted me to take it. As I grabbed his hand, he pulled me up and led me to the cell door. I thought to myself, *we'll never get out of here because the door is locked.* He proceeds to open the door, and we walk out of the cell. At that point, I'm thinking *that door was unlocked the whole time?* We walked down this dark and dreary hallway, and I was amazed at how many cells there were and how many people were trapped in this place of hopelessness.

Holding his hand, he took me up a flight of stairs, through another door, that brought us into an enormous building, where heat and stench were very heavy in the air. Everyone in this building is working so feverously, making weapons to destroy the world. I remember there being a red haze in the air. I found it strange because this was the first time I'd seen color in this vision. The creatures making the tools of destruction were not human. They were frightening, menacing powerful entities. I was scared that at any moment, they would notice me and throw me back down into the cell, under this factory of destruction. My guide looked back at me, as if to encourage me so that I would keep walking. As we continued to walk, I feared for my life, and I began to look down, hoping that nobody would see us. As I looked down, I saw a deadly snake that slithered towards us, and I knew that if this snake were to bite either one of us, we would die. I squeezed my Guide's hand to warn him of the danger that was coming our way. He turned around, looked at the snake with no fear in his eyes and kept on walking forward. I was terrified. Didn't he see what was about to happen?

We walked past the snake and it began to coil up into the pouncing position. I was about to pass the snake when it jumped out and tried to pierce the back of my foot. To my surprise, when the snake tried to bite me, its fangs bounced off and it knew it could not hurt me, and it slithered away. I remember thinking, *what just happened? This is impossible. I should be dead.*" My Guide just looked back at me with a kind smile, as if to say, "Don't worry, everything will be OK". Something changed in me, and I knew that he was more than just a Guide. It was as if He had the power that no other human being possessed. He made me feel safe and secure, hope was taking root. My Guide was leading me out of the pit of despair and hopelessness.

We came across a tall flight of stairs, and we began to climb them. As we were climbing to the top, I noticed a door. When we reached the door, my Guide opened it. I wish I could put into words all the senses that came to life as he showed me the other side. I could see that the sky was a crystal blue with white fluffy clouds, and they drifted eastward, on a warm, spring day. The birds were chirping, and there was a large row of trees lining the rolling meadow. In front of me was a field where you could run, skip, dance, and feel the warm breeze encircled around you. I walked through the door, and as I turned back to thank my Guide for leading me out of prison to a place of peace and happiness ... he was gone and my vision ended.

I am so thankful for this vision that God gave me as it gives me understanding of what the cross means to me. The dirt cell under the factory represents a place of hopelessness, or to me, a place I call "hell". I was captured by my own sin, and I lived in a place where I didn't know how to escape. In that cell, you have no dreams or strength to live. There is no color, comfort or life to be found. But when Jesus (my Guide) extended His hand ... I had to make a decision whether to take it or not. You see, God is always reaching; we're just not willing to trust that His desired plan for us is better than the desired plan we have for ourselves. When Jesus entered the cell without knowing it, I knew He brought hope to a hopeless situation. He never said a word to me. There was never any condemnation or anger for being in that cell. He just held out His hand with love and compassion and waited for me to grab it. When you take His hand to lead you ... your life changes forever.

I was beginning to connect the Word of God and prayer. God was speaking to me through the Spirit and giving me understanding of who He was and what He wanted to do for me and my life. I was at a new level of faith, which demanded I trust that He was real, and most importantly, that He was alive in my life. The vision had given me revelation of who Jesus really was. He was my Savior, someone whom I could put my trust in. I was beginning to believe that He was One I could trust would take care of me and make everything ok. I had hope, again, to believe in the goodness of God and the chance for a new life. Joy began to bubble up inside of me. What did the Lord have planned for my life? The possibilities were endless. I was beginning to dream again and experience a freedom within my spirit.

"You have turned my mourning into joyful dancing. You have taken away my clothes of mourning and clothed me with joy." (Psalm 30:11)

It amazed me that the God of the Universe, the One who made all things would take the time to reveal to me His love and His Word in action, so that I could understand the depth of the affection that He had for me. The revelation that He showed me that day was that there's no place you can go to that He cannot reach. I was making a connection with the God of the universe, and when I began to search for Him, through the word and through prayer, He showed me things that were hidden to me in the past. There is truly joy in His presence.

"Taste and see that the LORD is good. Oh, the joys of those who take refuge in him!" (Psalm 34:8 NLT)

In the movie "Hope Floats" Sandra Bullocks character makes it through the humiliation and shame of a divorce. She makes a decision for her daughter's sake and begins to live again. She walks down a path of self-discovery as a different person in her hometown. Humbled by her past, she allows time to heal her broken heart, so that she and her daughter can begin to live again, and by the end of the movie, love begins to bloom with an old boyfriend. She takes a risk and begins to hope that true love really exists.

I was at a point in my marriage where I needed something to change, or I would completely lose my identity and fall back into the pit of depression. Through this vision, I was given hope that true love really existed. It gave me focus and strength to continue praying and reading the Word of God so that I would know more of this unconditional love that was pursuing me. I was coming alive with hope, and vigor for life, and I wanted to share it with those I loved.

(I want to take this moment to enlighten my readers: If you feel shame or guilt from your past, and if it is telling you that you can never change or that the reality of your decisions has not lead you to a place of fulfillment, and you feel trapped in a dying relationship, there is still hope. That hope is Jesus Christ. He is the One who can take an impossible situation, and make it possible again. He is waiting for you to ask him to come into your heart, but you first need to ask for forgiveness of your sins. The Bible says: We all have fallen short of the glory of God, meaning we are all sinners. This is not a surprise to Jesus, for that was the reason he came to the earth and died on a cross, that our sins could be forgiven. After you've asked for forgiveness, tell Him that you want Him to be the Lord and Savior of your life. Take His hand and He will lead you out of your sickness, sadness and/or frustration. All it takes is faith in His Word and a humble heart to follow in His ways. Trust Him to do what He said He would do. He will fill you with His hope, and you will experience joy and peace that will overflow by the power of the Holy Spirit)

Chapter Six

Learning New Steps

*"Dear brothers and sisters, when troubles come your
way, consider it an opportunity for great joy." James 1:2*

The miraculous way in which hugging works is
described in a touching story titled, 'The Hugging Judge',
in *Chicken Soup for the Soul,* by Jack Canfield and Mark
Victor Hansen. It is about Lee Shapiro, a retired judge,
who realized that love is the greatest power there is and
began offering everybody a hug.

Some years ago, he created the Hugger Kit. It contains
30 little red embroidered hearts. Shapiro would take out
his kit, go around to people, and offer them a little red
heart in exchange for a hug. Soon, he became a minor
celebrity for spreading his message of unconditional
love.

Once accepting a challenge from a local television
station in San Francisco, he went ahead and offered a hug
to a six-foot-two, 230-pound bus driver, from a
community known to be the toughest, crabbiest and
meanest person in the whole town. As the TV cameras

captured the footage, the bus driver stepped down and said: "Why not?"

Shapiro was then invited to a home for the terminally ill, severely retarded and quadriplegics. Accompanied by a team of doctors and nurses, he went about his routine of hugging and handing out little red hearts until they reached a ward with the worst cases. The last person, named Leonard, whom Shapiro had to hug, was drooling on his big white bib; *how am I going to communicate love to him,* Shapiro thought. Finally, he leaned down and gave Leonard a hug. This is what followed, in the authors' words:

All of a sudden Leonard began to squeal: "Eeeeehh! Eeeeehh!" Some of the other patients in the room began to clang things together. Shapiro turned to the staff for some sort of explanation, only to find that every doctor, nurse and orderly was crying. Shapiro asked the head nurse: "What's going on?" Shapiro will never forget what she said: "This is the first time in 23 years we've ever seen Leonard smile.[1]

There is nothing like a mother's hug. In my mother's arms, I always felt safe, and secure, from all the world's problems and concerns. She was the one and only person, that seemed to know me better than myself, and could recognize when I needed one. She was my source of strength, whenever I was scared, she was always there when I needed a friend.

I'm not sure when the hugs stopped in my life with my mom, but I do remember when the feeling of security ended: When my sister died. As I look back, I am able to see that the lack of forgiveness and bitterness towards my parents was erroneous. I am also thankful to God that even when we sinned, He's able to bring reconciliation to our relationships. As a parent now, I understand they were doing their best to encourage me, even though I didn't recognize it.

It is amazing to me that God shows His glory in the midst of trials, and if we are to allow Him to lead our lives, He will take us out of the darkness and bring us through to his marvelous light. It says in the bible:

"And we know that God causes everything to work together[1] for the good of those who love God and are called according to his purpose for them." (Romans 8:28 NLT)

At the age of fifty-one, my mom was diagnosed with Alzheimer's. News like this can shake your world. My family refused to believe the diagnosis until she started doing things that were out of character. I look back and wonder how we could possibly deny the obvious. Mom uncharacteristically lost her job due to poor job performance. If you knew my mom, you would know that she was a dedicated, punctual and hard working. Her termination was a shock. Then she started forgetting appointments. As time went on, we knew that something was wrong. Being a nurse for twenty-seven years, Mom was very aware that she was showing all the signs of Alzheimer's. Not wanting to worry us, she would try to hide her forgetfulness by joking around or laughing it off. Pretty soon, it wasn't funny anymore.

Mom would buy items at the store, get home, and not be able to find them. She'd struggle to remember what she did with her purchase. There were times that she would cook something on the stovetop and forget about it. Other times, she would drive to a friend's home, only twenty minutes away, only to discover she'd take an hour trying to find her way; my mom was getting lost in familiar territory.

The family confronted dad about the strange behaviors and pleaded with him to take her to her doctor. Maybe this was the early stages; maybe there was a cure that could stop this while it was still new. Dad denied the severity of the quick progression and wouldn't accept the fact that there was no easy answer to the fate that might lay before him. The woman that he loved was slowly degenerating, her mind dying a little bit every day. As far as he knew, the doctors couldn't give him any hope for a cure.

My dad was forty-nine years old with two adult sons and one teenage daughter at home. Eric and I lived about 40 minutes away from my Dad so it made visits difficult. I wrote in my journal 10/22/1998:

I prayed today, and I asked God if I should ask my dad if he would allow my mother to come over once a week so that we could spend some time together. As I thought about this idea, the Lord showed me an image of a rainbow in my mind. I remember the story of Noah's ark from the Bible, in which a rainbow was used as a promise from God that He would not flood the earth again. I believe that this "rainbow" is God's way of saying "yes" to me, and that He is keeping this promise. Because I have not always allowed my mother into my life, I still feel like I want to help her through this difficult time. Although I miss the mom that I once knew, I know that it is not too late to allow her back into my life. I also prayed that God would help me to be a good daughter.

We all go through seasons in our life. Some are easy; some not. Seasons mean change. Fall symbolizes letting go of things and allowing them to drop from the branches of life. It's closing a chapter and moving to the next one. Change isn't always easy as I was about to find out.

Chapter Seven

Practice, Practice, Practice

*"But those who trust in the LORD will find new strength.
They will soar high on wings like eagles. They will run
and not grow weary. They will walk and not faint."*
Isaiah 40:3

I find it interesting how quickly we change when
we're filled with God's love, and we begin to have a
desire to love those around us. When I wrote this entry in
my journal, it was only one day after I had repented of
my sins and asked God to help me to stop drinking. God's
miraculous touch in my life immediately sparked
something in my heart: To give back to those I loved.
God gave me the love and compassion to step out in
faith, believe that I could do something for my mother,
and help my dad in this trying situation. It says in the
Bible:

*"Trust in the LORD with all your heart; do not depend on
your own understanding. ⁶ Seek his will in all you do, and
he will show you which path to take." (Proverbs 3:5-6
NLT)*

I was going to surrender my will to God and trust in His strength. I was experiencing a goodness inside of me, which gave me strength to love those who were in my life. It became easier to care for my family as they began to notice the difference in me. God's love was growing inside of me and I was being transformed into someone who was more loving, gentle and giving.

Don't get me wrong: I didn't instantly become wife and mother of the year. I had my struggles with carnality, but I began to have a clearer understanding of what was right and wrong in God's eyes. I knew that when I did something wrong that didn't please God that peace within my spirit would leave me. Once you taste the peace of God in your life, you never want to go back to the stress of this world. In the Bible, Jesus says:

"I am leaving you with a gift—peace of mind and heart. And the peace I give is a gift the world cannot give. So don't be troubled or afraid." (John 14:27 NLT)

For the next eleven years, I saw my mother progressively decline in her ability to communicate and perform daily functions. Praise God that He gave my father the wisdom and strength to go through this ordeal with love and respect for her. He showed me what a true husband looks like. Not just by his words but by his actions. He made a promise to her when they got married: That he would love her in sickness and in health until death due them part, and he kept it. My dad never showed self-pity. He held his head up high even when he was slowing down, and others were pulling away from them.

My father did hours of research in hopes that the latest testing and drug on the market might prolong her life. He also realized that taking care of Mom was going to be a full-time job. Knowing that, Dad retired so that he could stay home and take care of the love of his life. I admire him for his faithfulness and unselfish attitude of not putting any of the burden on his children. Here was an example of an amazing man: Exemplifying incredible love and care for my mom. I thank God for him in my life.

Through this trial, God brought reconciliation between my mother and I. We would go shopping at the mall and look for bargains. In fact, at the beginning stages, Mom would forget where she parked the car at the mall. It used to frustrate her so much. There were times she'd set a package down and forget to pick it up and walk away. When we'd shop for clothes, Mom would take an outfit into the dressing room and come out to show me, only to discover she put it on backwards or inside out. When she realized that she had forgotten something or made a mistake, the overwhelming flood of emotion would bring her to tears. God then gave me the love and words of encouragement for her to push past the emotions and to be grateful for the time we had together.

There was one particular moment I'll never forget: We were shopping and Mom was suddenly overcome with the reality of her situation. She looked at me with tears in her eyes and said, "You are an angel that God has given me to help me through my fears, and I am grateful that you are my child." I remember that those words gave me strength to endure through this trial. Even though I couldn't fix the situation, I still had a purpose in her life, and God was allowing me to be a part of it. I wasn't afraid of death like I was when my sister was sick. Why? Because, by that point, I had a friend that was stronger than me, and his name is Jesus. Even though God was not choosing to heal her mind from Alzheimer's, He was allowing this trial to bring reconciliation between us. In my journal entry from 11/11/1998, I wrote:

"Yesterday my mother and I touched souls. She told me that she really loved me. She held me in her arms so tight and cried. I felt like she was saying good-bye to me."

My mother would live the next ten years in her home, and although it was hard to watch my mother slowly shut down, it helped us as a family to appreciate our time together. Life is a gift from God, and sometimes, we forget how valuable we are to one another … and to Him. I was blessed that God gave me the time to restore my relationship with my mother before she died. When I was a child, she was my strength and my protection from people that would try to harm me, either physically or with words. She taught me how to care for myself and others through respect and kindness. Mom showed me how to believe in God and be obedient to him, how to sacrifice and give from the heart so that others could experience joy.

Trials are not easy to go through and most of time, you can't see the purpose or reason. This is where you need to depend on a little thing called faith. The Bible says:

"And it is impossible to please God without faith."
(Hebrews 11:6 NLT)

Trials are tests of our faith in God to prevail in preserving ourselves until His return. Just because we are Christians doesn't mean we'll never feel pain or sorrow. Scripture says:

"I have told you all this so that you may have peace in me. Here on earth you will have many trials and sorrows. But take heart, because I have overcome the world."

(John 16:33 NLT)

The Christian life is a process: you give God all your sins and problems, and He begins to bring out the best in you. Because of the works of the cross, you receive God's grace and forgiveness so that you are able to get back up and live obediently to the Spirit. You can't "earn" God's peace or love, but you do have to ask Him for His forgiveness for your sins, and accept Him as your Savior. Upon that acceptance, you receive God's promise. He said: If you ask for forgiveness of sin in your life, He will forgive you and wash you clean because of the works of the cross; then you simply believe His promises are true. God knows everything about you and regardless of your past, he still loves you. You don't need to hide from Him or think He is mad at you. If you can embrace this idea and believe it, He will lead you out of darkness and into His marvelous light.

In Jesus' message, he's telling us to take courage in spite of the inevitable struggles we'll face. He will not leave us, nor forsake us. Jesus does not abandon us during our struggles either. We need to remember that the ultimate victory has already been won, and that we can claim the peace of Christ in the most troublesome times. We can truly count it as joy when we fall into trials for it grows our faith in the One who can bring us victory from death.

Chapter Eight

Did I Pick the Right Dance Partner?

"And it is impossible to please God without faith. Anyone who wants to come to him must believe that God exists and that he rewards those who sincerely seek him."
Hebrews 11:6

A man from Norfolk, VA, called a local radio station to share this on Sept 11th, 2003, TWO YEARS AFTER THE TRAGEDIES OF 9/11/2001. His name was Robert Matthews. These are his words:

A few weeks before Sept. 11th, my wife and I found out that we were going to have our first child, so she planned a trip out to California, to visit her sister. On our way to the airport, we prayed that God would grant her a safe trip and that He would be with her. Shortly after I said Amen, we both heard a loud pop and then the car shook violently. We had blown out a tire. I replaced the tire as quickly as I could, but we still missed her flight. Both of us were very upset as we drove home.

I received a call from my father, who was retired from the NYFD, and he asked me what my wife's flight number was, but I explained that we had missed the flight.

My father informed me, that her flight number was the one that crashed into the southern tower. I was too shocked to speak, as my father was telling me of more news; that he was going to help. "This is not something I can just sit by for. I have to do something." I was concerned for his safety, of course, but more because he had never given his life to Christ. So, after a brief debate, I knew that his mind was made up, so he said, "Take good care of my grandchild". Those were the last words I ever heard my father say, because he died while helping in the rescue effort.

My joy, that my prayer of safety for my wife had been answered quickly, but I still became angry. I was angry at God, at my father, and at myself. I had gone for nearly two years blaming God for taking my father away, and now My son would never know his grandfather. My father had never accepted Christ, and I never got to say good-bye.

Then something happened. About two months ago, I was sitting at home with my wife and my son, when there was a knock on the door. I looked at my wife, but I could tell she wasn't expecting anyone. I opened the door to a couple with a small child.

The man looked at me and asked if my father's name was Jake Matthews. I told him it was and he quickly grabbed my hand and said, "I never got the chance to meet your father, but it is an honor to meet his son." He explained to me, that his wife had worked in the World Trade Center , and had been caught inside after the attack. She was pregnant and had been caught under debris. He then explained that my father had been the one to find his wife and free her. My eyes welled up with tears, as I thought of my father giving his life for people like this. He then said, "There is something else you need to know." His wife then told me, that as my father worked to free her, she talked to him and led him to Christ. I began sobbing at the news.1

When their baby boy was born, they named him Jacob Matthews, in honor of the man who gave his life so that a mother and baby could live.1

I love to hear stories, or testimonies, of God's greatness and divine truth, that He is in control. It says in the Bible,

"For your kingdom is an everlasting kingdom. You rule throughout all generations. The LORD always keeps his promises; he is gracious in all he does." (Psalm 145:13 NLT)

My finite mind cannot wrap itself around the idea that God, who made the whole universe and sets everything in motion would want to spend time with me. In fact, the Bible states: He wants to show me His plan for my life. It sounds crazy, but it's true!

I would like to share two testimonies: The first testimony explains how quickly God answers prayer, and the second, explains how God taught me to wait on His timing as He laid the groundwork for a ministry I would become involved in.

Six months after I determined to give God my entire life, I developed a steady discipline of prayer and reading of the Word. As a result, my life progressively got better. There was lightness in my heart, and I had more love and patience for my children and husband. Furthermore, they began to see this in me. Bear in mind, my kids were the only ones, at this point, that knew about this new relationship and journey I had with God.

I knew from my past experiences that if I was going to stay committed, I needed to set some goals. Without fail, you will always face opposition when you walk in faith and trust in God.

My first goal was that every morning, I would read three chapters in the Bible. Once I finished, I would go into my bedroom to spend time with God. I was so serious about this that I told my kids, "Unless you're bleeding, do not disturb me while I pray." I would go as far as turning off the ringer on our home phone so that nobody would disturb my time with God.

At the very beginning of my walk, I never heard God audibly speak to me, although He would encourage me through visual images in my mind. On one occasion, He revealed to me small visions about random things. These visions always intrigued me because I've always loved puzzles. It made me feel like I was on an exciting journey to discover who I was in Jesus and what God had planned for me. These snapshots or visions, if you will, encouraged me to press on in my quest to know who God is. God says in His Word:

"In the last days,' God says, 'I will pour out my Spirit upon all people. Your sons and daughters will prophesy. Your young men will see visions, and your old men will dream dreams." (Acts 2:17 NLT)

His Word and His Spirit were leading me on a new road of faith, and doors opened so that I could exercise these truths. I wrote in my journal on November 13, 1998:

I felt God's love surge through my fingers, arms and into my body. It was a warm tingling fluent sensation. It gave me a feeling of God's power in my life. I also saw in my mind, a beautiful boutique of red tulips. (One of my favorite flowers) I feel that he is trying to say, "He is glad that we are together."

I couldn't keep this love encounter all to myself just like when you find an unbelievable bargain at a store, you will stop at nothing to share the good news, calling all your friends and stopping strangers to share your miraculous find. The only difference between a great sale and sharing God's love is that a sale is easy to believe because you know that stores and products exist. When it comes to sharing the Gospel, however, it's a bit different. First you have to believe or have faith that God exists, and that He longs to reveal himself to you. It says in Hebrews 11:6:

"And it is impossible to please God without faith. Anyone who wants to come to him must believe that God exists and that he rewards those who sincerely seek him."
(Hebrews 11:6 NLT)

Many times it's easier to talk to total strangers than the ones you love the most. I decided to take a huge leap of faith and talk to my nine-year-old daughter, Courtney. She was well aware of who Jesus was and what He did on the cross for her. At that point, she was attending a Catholic elementary school. She had such a childlike faith and was a very obedient child. Courtney trusted me, and I was about to open a whole new world to her. Because Courtney had some basic Christian knowledge, I was able to share the Word of God with her, telling her that if she would just be still, God would reveal himself to her.

As I look back at my journal entry on November 5, 1998, I wrote:

I told Courtney about what I was doing in my bedroom when I prayed, and I asked her if she would like to try it? She said, "Yes", and when she was done waiting on God, she told me about what she saw. God had taken her on an exciting journey. Lord, thank you for showing me that I am not crazy in my time of prayer.

The more time I spent with God, the more He shared with me. I don't think I can convey enough how special this time was. Before this point, I'd lost trust in so many people and had deeply desired a relationship where I could pour myself into and in return feel safe and grow. My time with God was meeting all those desires. The more time I spent with Him, the more I wanted to share His love.

I now got to a point where I needed to share this joy with my husband. He knew that I was reading the Bible everyday, and he was beginning to see my changed life. The challenging part of this was that we never had any deep discussions on what was happening in my life when I prayed and waited on God. Eric would listen intently and receive the reality of my experiences, but deep down, I sensed his skepticism. Eric knew his Bible better than anyone else I knew. He had always felt a calling on his life but had essentially ignored it. I was always amazed at how Eric could talk about biblical topics and sound so knowledgeable. I realized, however, that what I was sharing with him was not being received as scriptural material but relational material. This was always an area of struggle for Eric. I thought that since he was at least willing to listen, maybe God would put a hunger in his heart to discover a relationship like the newfound one I had developed with Him. I wrote in my journal on November 27, 1998:

Yesterday I shared with Eric, what God had revealed to me in prayer, so that if he were to pray to God, he would be encouraged and so that God could help him. This made him angry and he mocked me for believing that God could really talk to you. Why did he act like he believed me when he didn't? I thought that he saw the changes that had taken place in me and that he was proud of how I trusted God. He made me so mad, that I chose to recoil back into my selfish ways, and became someone whom I didn't like. God forgive me. Did I marry the wrong man?

Never in my life had I ever questioned whether Eric was the man that God had created for me. I remember that on our second date, I had looked him in the eyes and told him, "I'm going to marry you someday", and for a split second, his eyes grew larger, and he said, "Really?" He looked me in the eyes and for a moment, he didn't know what to say, but he recovered from the bold statement that I made and said, "I'll bet you're right!" I, honestly, don't know what came over me at that moment, but I just knew that he was going to be my husband, and when I let that thought out of my heart, I knew that he believed me, and I waited two and half years for it to come to pass.

So for me to write in my journal or question in my spirit that Eric was the right man for me proved that God was beginning to have a strong influence on my life. He had become the one whom I trusted with my problems and concerns, and He was my source of wisdom and strength. He was my friend and my confidant when I was searching for answers. He was my joy and hope for receiving any wholeness and healing. I knew by faith that God cared and wanted Him to reveal the answer to my question: Was Eric the one? I was about to get my answer.

Chapter Nine

Dancing With Others

"For I hold you by your right hand— I, the LORD your God. And I say to you, 'Don't be afraid. I am here to help you." Isaiah 41:13

There is nothing more exciting or invigorating when God answers your prayers. The very next day, Eric came home from work early and poured out his heart: "I want a deeper relationship with you, and I want to be your soul mate. I have seen a change in you, and I know it's because of your relationship with God." This was such a relief in my heart. Eric believed and appreciated the change in me. Sometimes we don't always know how God does it, but He is an on-time God. Eric gave me a tiny, wrapped box. To my surprise, I found a necklace. Not an ordinary necklace, but a Mitzpah necklace. Mitzpah in Hebrew means a commandment of the Jewish law or a worthy deed. The necklace was in the shape of a heart that was divided down the middle, creating two separate necklaces and inscribed on the back with the following scripture:

"May the LORD keep watch between us to make sure that we keep this covenant when we are out of each other's sight." (Genesis 31:49 NLT)

He told me that if I ever felt lonely or needed a reminder of his love for me that I was just to look at the necklace and know that his heart was with me. I knew this was God because it was not like Eric to be so vulnerable and transparent. I believe that my husband was sensing that my heart was changing, and that he had to make a decision as to whether he was going to let me go or if he was going to try to understand my relationship with God. The Lord was showing me the power of His love by answering my prayer, which according to His Word says:

"Since they are no longer two but one, let no one split apart what God has joined together." (Matthew 19:6 NLT).

God's Spirit was working through both my husband and I to draw us closer to each other and ultimately to God. The Lord had answered my prayer and confirmed that Eric was the man for me.

Praise God! My heart was at rest in God's love and excited about this new hope of a deeper relationship with my husband. I felt a sense of security with Eric and a peace with God that I had never known. Experiencing God's glory changes our perspective of who God is and how He can change the circumstances of our life if we just ask. God's joy fills you with a desire to sing God's praises; it also empowers you to want to help someone who's struggling or in need of encouragement. I was learning that God's love will give you the strength and compassion to reach out to someone who is hurting with no regards to the cost or sacrifice of your own life.

The second manifestation of God's glory in my life was when I began to dream again. My faith was skyrocketing at this point, and I was longing to give myself to God with all of my heart no matter the cost. The Bible reads: *He takes us from glory to glory. (2 Corinthians 3:18)* My faith in God's power to do the impossible was breaking down strongholds in my mind. My doubts and fears were being replaced with new possibilities. In my spirit, God was telling me that my words mattered to Him, and He was ready to fulfill His dream for my life. There's a Bible verse that strengthens me when I'm in doubt and fear comes knocking on my door, and it reads:

"Humanly speaking, it is impossible. But with God everything is possible." (Matthew 19:26 NLT)

God was about to open my understanding of his love for people and use that understanding for His glory.

At this time, I was attending a Catholic Church in Milwaukee. The priest was extremely charismatic: He had the ability to preach a sermon by painting a picture in your mind of how God works in your life through the Scriptures. The choir director was from California and had attended seminary with him. He was musically gifted and ministered it through new songs that were filled with praise and worship. With these two men working together, something was changing in the church, and in turn, people were telling their friends about it and the church grew.

One Sunday morning, I was sitting behind a woman in her early thirties, who had four young children under eight. You could tell that she cared about her children, and that she taught them the importance of attending church, but her two youngest ones had a hard time sitting still. During the service, there were multiple times she had to correct the youngest ones. After she had got done correcting them, they were back at it again, being disruptive. You could tell that she wanted to hear the message that was coming over the pulpit, but her attention was focused on controlling the kids and not the message. I wanted to help her, but she didn't know me. So as I was watching her struggle, a thought came into my mind: *We really needed a nursery in this church.*

Next Sunday, I decided to sit in a different part of the church. She wanted to hear the message, so did I. Her kids were distracting and made it hard for me to be ministered too. Be careful when you become self-centered and not others-centered. God has a way of correcting you.

I sat down, excited to worship and get fed by the man of God. I watched for the woman with the children, but she hadn't arrive. I was hoping she wouldn't notice I moved. The service was about to begin, and wouldn't you just know it, the woman and her kids walked in. Not only did they show up, but they decided to try sitting in a different pew also ... right next to me! Again, halfway through the service, the two younger ones started acting up, and my heart began to break for this mother. I could see that she was embarrassed, but she still chose to keep the kids in the service. I wished there was some way to help her, but I felt helpless. Then a thought came to me, *it sure would be nice to have a nursery for those kids.* This time God went a step further and said, *sure would be nice if you started a nursery so that woman would have some place to send her kids.* That thought couldn't be from God ... could it? I wanted to help her. I knew the nursery was the answer, but how could *I* make this happen?

I began to pray about it and asked God if this thought was from Him. One thing I have learned in discerning the will of God for my life is: When it's from the Spirit, and it lines up with the Word of God, the thought won't leave you. You can run from it, but God will not stop pursuing you as He wants you to trust Him so that He can accomplish His work through you. Once you surrender to His will, peace enters in, and He will keep you moving forward until whatever it is that He wants done is accomplished. So, needless to say, I surrendered to what He wanted me to do, and I started planning for a nursery.

I began to pray, "God, how do you want to do this?" A thought came to me, *I should start collecting toys every week by going to rummage sales and looking at clearance items from local stores.* I told Eric about my idea, and he told me to go for it. We weren't wealthy by any means, but God provided the money we needed to buy toys. As the collection of toys grew, I knew I needed to approach the priest to start this nursery. Furthermore, I would need a room in the school building, next to the church, to store the supplies.

I had been a stay-at-home mom for eight years, and my confidence to start a new project outside of the home terrified me. In my mind, my track record of not finishing big projects was pretty powerful. For instance, I had started nursing school when my first two children were young, and after two years, when I needed to enter into the clinical portion of the program, I realized it was too much, and I quit. Then, as the kids got older, the itch to get back into the workplace started calling me again. I had a real passion for interior design. So I went back to school and got my Interior Design Certification. I then find out it would only get me a job selling furniture and had little to do with designing rooms. Needless to say, after graduation, I never pursued getting a job because deep down, I never desired to be anything more than a wife and mother. Now there I was, and the Lord was asking me to start this nursery. Although I struggled with believing that I could organize and lead this ministry, Scripture was very clear in Luke 9:23:

"If any of you wants to be my follower, you must turn from your selfish ways, take up your cross daily, and follow me." (Luke 9:23 NLT)

Step one: Asking the priest if I could start a nursery. As much as I loved God, I was still new to the faith. I had a hard time believing that God really wanted to use me. How could I help love parents and their children? Deep down, I struggled with believing that this is what God wanted me to do.

The thought continued to stay in mind, so I finally wrote the Priest a letter. Several weeks passed, and he never mentioned that he'd received the letter and as our church continued to grow and as the noise level grew with more children coming in with their families, I became frustrated.

I was so sure that this thought had come from God. So I continued to walk in faith and collect toys at rummage sales. I would tell the people who were having these sales that the toys were being used for the nursery at our church. Here's how awesome God is as a provider: When I told people at rummage sales that, their demeanor would change, and they would give me discounts on the toys, some even gave me the toys for free! This was such an encouragement from the Lord. Eric was beginning to lose faith that this concept was from God and asked me to stop collecting toys. I can't blame him. I was spending his hard earned money, building a pile of toys in our basement that we didn't have room for, and the priest was not getting back to me. I decided to give it a few more days.

Unbeknownst to me at the time, the Priest had received the letter but was cautious about the idea because he thought I wanted to be paid for this ministry.

The reason the decision took so long was because he needed to take it to the church trustees for approval as to whether it was in the budget. I finally got a call from him, and he asked me if I could have the nursery set up by that Sunday. Let me just say, God is so faithful! As we talked, I told him that I had no intention of being paid. I was simply honoring what God wanted me to do. When God moves … God moves. I was so glad that I had listened to the Spirit. If I hadn't started collecting toys, there is no way I would have been ready to start that Sunday.

The church gave me the Kindergarten room in the school which was perfect because everything was designed for children. They provided a large hall closet so that I could store all the toys and not have to lug them in and out of the school each week. Here was the best part of the story: The two children who used to sit in front of me in church and misbehave were the first ones to walk into the nursery doors. God gave me peace that this was His will for my life at that time, and it was being confirmed. The burden that I was carrying was being released, and my faith in God to use me in a ministry was growing strong.

For the next two years, God provided all of the necessary supplies, staff and ideas, so that the children would grow in the knowledge of Jesus through songs, bible stories, and fellowship. It was a place where kids enjoyed going to church, and parents felt the support of a church family and the love of Christ. There was a purpose in waiting for God to fulfill the dream that he put in my heart for the nursery. He showed me that when my heart was right, He can use me to minister to others. He showed me that He can move on the hearts of those who are of higher authority in my life to help me achieve God's goals. He reminded me through the power of the Holy Spirit that: I was able to receive wisdom for each day and the strength to endure through troubled times with patience as I wait on God's timing. Only God can touch my heart in such a supernatural way; it happened when I saw those two little children and their mom coming to the nursery for the first time. God is truly our provider and strength in the good times and the bad times. He deserves all the glory. While waiting on His timing, it built my faith and my strength and it has shown me that whatever comes my way, God is there for me. Scripture says:

"What shall we say about such wonderful things as these? If God is for us, who can ever be against us?" (Romans 8:31 NLT)

Chapter Ten

Needing New Dance Shoes

The LORD replied, "I will personally go with you, Moses, and I will give you rest—everything will be fine for you." Exodus 33:14

Why is it that we have more faith in the pieces of a puzzle, made by a company in Taiwan, fitting together than we do in the pieces of our life presented to us by God? One person chooses to put like pieces together first, while another chooses to put the edges of the puzzle together first, but neither individual ever really doubts that the puzzle will somehow fit perfectly. The edges, in and of themselves, probably have little to do with the main image or idea of the puzzle. Yet without it, the puzzle is incomplete. In fact, although these pieces appear to have little to do with the main idea or image, they are nonetheless all just as important to the puzzle's completion. In the beginning, some pieces, even when fitted perfectly together, might not help you to understand what the puzzle is all about. It is only on its completion that you can appreciate the parts that at first seemed insignificant or pointless to be worthwhile. ı

I have to say, I do like puzzles because they have an element of discovery and challenge, and when you find two pieces that fit together, it gives you hope that you will get to the final result and see a beautiful picture. Walking by the Spirit is somewhat like putting a puzzle together. Just when you think you have discovered what God has in store for your life, He hands you a new piece and begins to open a new door of opportunity. God has created you for a purpose, and He holds all the pieces of the puzzle. Faith believes that all the pieces God gives you will fit together. If you'll just be patient and allow Him to give you one piece at a time, He will accomplish His purposes in your life.

God was about to hand me another puzzle piece. After six months of faithfully serving in the nursery ministry, I was nominated to sit on the Parish Council. The thought of being part of the leadership of the church and having a voice shocked me. I was used to leading a nursery with children, and now God wanted me to be a part of leading adults? I certainly wasn't looking for this, but I knew that God was challenging me to take another step of faith. When God called me to start the nursery, I questioned it and to some degree, fought the idea. This time, I decided to surrender. I knew that God was going to have His way, whether I liked it or not. There was a part of me that was willing to concede that maybe I wouldn't be chosen, and somebody else would get the position; then I would be off the hook. I was honored and thankful that someone in the church saw my dedication to the children and believed that I would be a good choice to serve as a leader of the church body.

The vote was taken and I got the nomination. I recognized that I didn't receive the position because I was the most talented or gifted person in the church, but because I was willing to trust God. I wanted to see the church grow.

The Parish Council consists of the Priest, two elected trustees and twelve representatives from the church body. As the governing body of the parish, the council oversees parish operations and budgets, as well as making advisory decisions on behalf of the parish. This was a great honor, and I was excited to continue as the nursery leader and ready for the new adventure God was opening up to me.

When I entered into my first Parish Council meeting, I was a little nervous and uncomfortable because I was not used to being involved in the business side of the church. I felt so inadequate and intimidated due to the fact that I didn't have any business education or secular experience, yet God placed me here. My meeting began with the Priest opening in prayer and a devotional. Next, we read the minutes from the last gathering and discussed changes that needed to be amended. After about an hour and a half, the Priest would ask for volunteers to accomplish tasks. The tasks were assigned, any additional business was discussed, and the meeting ended.

I served on the council for the next year and a half. I wish I could tell you that God was going to use me on the council for a long time, but He had other plans for my husband and I.

When I served on the council, the Catholic Archdiocese decided that during the 40 day period of lent, small groups would meet in homes to discuss a devotional that was approved by the Diocese. I was asked to lead one of the small groups that would meet during the day. My group consisted of an elderly couple, a newly divorced man, and myself. I thought there was something very special about this elderly couple because they had a love between them that transferred onto others. The husband was fighting against Alzheimer's, and the wife gave him the respect and honor due to his position, even with his illness. I don't think I've ever met anyone who handled their life with as much dignity and grace as she. It seemed there was never an unkind word that would exit her mouth. I noticed that in the church, she dedicated herself to sending out cards to people who needed a word of encouragement. There was something about her that made you feel good about yourself and made you want to be like her, and I could feel that.

They came faithfully for the study every week, and we started to get to know one another and sharing what God was doing in our lives. It just so happened that one of our studies was on the Holy Spirit. I shared with the wife that we had just received a bonus VHS, from a Biblical Leadership teaching series, on the Power of the Holy Spirit. She asked if she could borrow it. Since I believed that Eric and I had already received the Holy Spirit, there was no urgency for us to watch it. I handed her the video, and she took it home.

The following week, she returned the video to me and said that it was very good and thanked me for letting her borrow it. She had quite a few interesting things to say about the video and it peaked my interest. So after she left with her husband, I put the video into the machine, sat down on the couch and started to listen to what the teacher had to share. To my surprise, my life was about to change forever.

The teacher on the video began to share some Scripture of why we needed the Baptism of the Holy

Spirit. The Spirit gives us power to live an overcoming life and to be resurrected. (Acts 1:8, Romans 8:11) She went on to teach that belief in being filled with God's Spirit is not the same as the receiving of the Holy Spirit. That was a pretty bold statement. Now she'd captured my attention, or maybe God had. Where does it say what she was referring to in the Bible? Mark 16:17 it says:

"These miraculous signs will accompany those who believe: They will cast out demons in my name, and they will speak in new languages." (Mark 16:17 NLT)

I'd never heard this concept before, and I was curious as to what "tongues" or "new language" was and whether I could experience it. I never received any teaching like this before, but if it's in the Bible, it must be true. The troubling part of this video was that it appeared as though the teacher was telling me that if I didn't speak in tongues based on Mark 16:17, I didn't have the Holy Spirit living in me. Could there be more to what God wants to give me? She had my attention, and God was about to blow me away with this revelation.

Chapter Eleven

A Perfect Fit

"And everyone present was filled with the Holy Spirit and began speaking in other languages, as the Holy Spirit gave them this ability." Acts 2:4

As I continued to listen to her teach, she explained that God filled her until she overflowed with the joy of the Holy Spirit. She said, "At first, I struggled with allowing the Spirit to speak through me because I was trying to understand it, but the minute that I surrendered control of my tongue and allowed God's Spirit to move it, it flowed fluently."

She went on to teach about how to receive the Holy Spirit and said, "First, you need to ask God to forgive your sins because repentance empties you out, but God does not leave you empty because the Holy Ghost will fill you up; second, you must believe that God has forgiven you." It says in the Bible:

"But if we confess our sins to him, he is faithful and just

to forgive us our sins and to cleanse us from all wickedness." (1 John 1:9 NLT)

Finally, we need to pray and worship God and expect to receive the Holy Spirit. Speaking in tongues is a heavenly language that only God can give to you. So as you pray, your spirit speaks to God's Spirit in His language.

"For if I pray in tongues, my spirit is praying, but I don't understand what I am saying." (1 Corinthians 14:14 NLT)

The instructor continued by giving Scripture after Scripture that I needed to be filled with God's Holy Spirit with the evidence of speaking in tongues (Acts 10:44-46, Acts 2:1-4, Acts 19:6). I was convinced that I needed the Baptism of the Holy Spirit. When the teaching ended, I went into my bedroom, I shut the door, and I prayed. Now I asked God months ago to forgive me of my sins, but I wanted to do this in a Biblical way, so I started confessing to Him again. I told God that I believed He had forgiven me for my sins, and that I wanted to receive the Baptism of the Holy Spirit. I began to thank Him for what He had done for me, through the cross. I began to worship Him by telling Him how much I loved Him and then it happened: At first, just a few sounds came out of my mouth, but as I surrendered my spirit, it flowed through me like a spring. This is what Jesus meant when He said,

"Anyone who believes in me may come and drink! For the Scriptures declare, 'Rivers of living water will flow from his heart." [39] *(When he said "living water," he was speaking of the Spirit, who would be given to everyone believing in him. But the Spirit had not yet been given, because Jesus had not yet entered into his glory.)" (John 7:38-39 NLT)*

As incredible as this experience was, I lacked the knowledge of what I had just received. So instead of telling everyone the good news (that I had been filled with God's marvelous Spirit), I kept it to myself. I needed to trust the Bible to teach me and guide me. One of the things that was expressed in this teaching was the necessity of the infilling to receive salvation. Here was another challenging statement to my current belief system: According to the Word, speaking in tongues is a gift from God to give me power to witness effectively. Up to this point, I had no problem with this new wonderful gift God, in His grace, had given me. Based upon what was being taught and the Scriptures that were used to support the teaching, the infilling of the Holy Ghost was an essential piece of salvation. This seemed so absolute, as if there was no room for debate.

If you question the above, let me ease your concerns by presenting Scripture that confirms the need to be filled with the Holy Spirit, evidenced by speaking in tongues, as a salvation requirement.

First we need a little history about the New Testament covenant that God revealed through the Apostle Peter. The Book of Acts was the first book to be written after Jesus' ascension, and it was written by Luke the physician. Its purpose is to give an accurate account of the birth and growth of the early Christian Church. It links Christ's life to the life of the church; the Gospels to the New Testament Epistles.

From the very beginning, Jesus tells his apostles and followers to wait in Jerusalem for the promise of the Holy Spirit (Acts 1:8). They didn't know what it meant to receive the promise of the Holy Spirit, but because Jesus told them to wait, they did. On the day of Pentecost (ten days after Jesus told them to wait), they were all gathered together in one room. The Holy Spirit came upon them, and they were all filled with the Holy Ghost, evidenced by speaking in an unknown language called "tongues" (Acts 2:1-4). At this time, there were Jews from many nations gathered, and they heard the apostles speaking their own respective language and were amazed because they were all Galileans. Peter boldly delivers his first sermon about God's salvation plan for the world.

His sermon outlined who Jesus was and how they missed the fact that He was the Messiah. They accused Him of blasphemy and sentenced Him to crucifixion. Upon this revelation, the people were convicted that they had killed their Messiah, and fearing God's wrath, asked what they needed to do to be saved. Peter responded:

" Peter replied, "Each of you must repent of your sins and turn to God, and be baptized in the name of Jesus Christ for the forgiveness of your sins. Then you will receive the gift of the Holy Spirit." (Acts 2:38 NLT)

Now I read that and said to myself, "It doesn't say anything about tongues in Acts 2:38." But when I went back and looked at Acts 2:4, which read, "And they were all *filled with the Holy Ghost* and *began to speak with other tongues* as the Spirit gave them the utterance", it made sense that when Peter told them they'd receive the gift of the Holy Spirit, they would speak with other tongues. It goes together logically.

If you're still not convinced that speaking in tongues is the evidence of being filled with the Holy Spirit, let me share this Scripture which settles the issue for me: Acts 2:33 says:

"Now he is exalted to the place of highest honor in heaven, at God's right hand. And the Father, as he had

promised, gave him the Holy Spirit to pour out upon us, just as you see and hear today." (Acts 2:33 NLT)

Through what these people and others like them were able to see and hear, God gave them evidence of baptism in the Holy Ghost. What did they see and hear? They **heard and saw** people speaking in tongues.

The Bible tells us that Jesus Christ is the same yesterday, today and forever (Hebrews 13:8). According to the Word of God, Jesus does not change his plan or try to confuse us about how to receive salvation. It is up to us to believe the Word of God, obey His instructions and by His grace, receive the Holy Spirit. Receiving the Holy Spirit is not a work which you can boast about; it is something that takes faith in the Word of God to receive it. My prayer for you today is that while you're reading this book, you will open your heart to Jesus, believe the Word of God and receive His free gift of salvation for your life.

Chapter Twelve

Signing Up for a Dance Class

"Above all, you must realize that no prophecy in Scripture ever came from the prophet's own understanding." 2 Peter 1:20

When this happened to me in my bedroom, I didn't have the understanding that I just shared with you, so I kept it to myself. Eric was starting to get involved in church affairs. He joined the Finance Committee and assisted in other areas of church life. Eric was changing before my eyes. He was not only reading the Word of God, but he started writing Bible lessons. These weren't just 8-10 page lessons either; he would write on Basic Christian Discipline, Stewardship and other topics where you could read from 30-50 pages on one lesson. Like I said, something was happening to him. The more he studied the Word, the more I saw him measure the actions of the church by the Word of God. I don't think it was judgment as much as it was trying to understand why certain things were done and others weren't. The original priest (who I've made previous mentions of throughout the reading), had left to take another parish. We got a new priest who was dramatically different than the first. Eric started getting frustrated that what was spoken at the pulpit didn't match God's Word.

One afternoon, Eric told me there were two reasons he was struggling with the church: 1.) the doctrinal values; and 2.) the vision for the future.

The first issue dealt with the church wanting Eric to serve as a trustee on the Board due to his involvement and experience in finance. In order to serve as a trustee, you need to be Catholic. Eric was raised Episcopalian and had no interest in becoming Catholic. The priest asked Eric if he'd like to go through the classes necessary to become Catholic. Eric politely declined, and said he understood that rules are rules and being on the Board was no big deal. But the priest was willing to circumvent the rules by neglecting to inform the powers that be that Eric wasn't Catholic so that Eric could serve as a trustee. His willingness to knowingly break rules in order to get his way bothered Eric. Further, this wasn't a parishioner suggesting this but the priest of the church.

The second reason was of greater concern: Eric had noticed several impoverished children, playing in the "projects", across the street from the church. Ministry has always been about "reaching our neighbors". For some reason, these kids that Eric saw across the street had an effect on him. Who was reaching out to them? Who was speaking to them about the love of God? One Sunday, Eric was standing out in front of the church with the priest. Looking across the street, he asked him about the impoverished children and their families that were living there. He wanted to know if the church had made an effort to reach out to them. It seemed like it was a natural question to ask since they were right across the street from the church. The priest didn't answer. Eric didn't know what to say. He couldn't believe that this man of God was content not to reach out to those less fortunate in his own backyard. Eric was ready to turn a corner in his walk with God, but he needed someone's help. He couldn't explain it, but he knew that he wasn't going to find it at this church, and so Eric's long spiritual journey began.

I was becoming extremely involved with the church. I was running the nursery, sitting on Parish Council and facilitating a small group. All this involvement was giving me purpose, and I felt I was being used by God. Eric, on the other hand, was so unhappy. He literally was reaching the point of depression. He was searching so hard for answers, for completeness, for peace. Finally I told him, "If you find a church that follows the Bible, I'll leave here and go with you." I wasn't very concerned about him finding a new church because all Christian churches were the same … right?

For months, I continued to stay involved and attend our church while Eric was on his spiritual quest. He visited Lutheran, Methodist, Baptist, and Non-Denominational churches. He not only attended a Jewish Synagogue, but even a church with oriental markings on the front sign that grabbed his attention. He searched and searched, but he wasn't finding what he was looking for. Ironically, one of his employee's father was a Pastor. Eric was pretty open about his faith, and this employee knew he was searching for a church. So she invited him to her father's service. Her father was pastor of a United Pentecostal Church, and one Sunday, Eric figured he had nothing to lose so he went to see what it was all about.

He wasn't very impressed when he pulled into the parking lot. The church was meeting in a school gymnasium. He walked in and took a seat in the back and waited for the service to begin. As the singing started, he realized something was radically different because people were lifting their hands and worshipping God. He later told me that he couldn't put his finger on it, but he felt that their worship was genuine. After several visits, Eric would leave before the sermon was preached. There was something about being in there that made Eric uncomfortable. Finally, he stayed one Sunday long enough to hear the sermon. As the Pastor preached, God began to convict him in his heart. The message seemed to be directed right at him. Being the skeptic that Eric can be, he wondered if his employee was telling her dad about his life. The message was so dead-on … so much so that Eric got up and left.

What's amazing is that as uncomfortable as that sermon made Eric feel, he continued to go every Sunday. During the week, the pastor started to take an interest in Eric and ask him out to lunch. The Pastor learned that Eric had written some bible studies, some well over 100 pages long, and he became intrigued. Eric told him about one in particular that he had done on the Holy Spirit and asked him if he could take a look at it. Eric gave him the study, and after the pastor had read it, they met again. The Pastor complimented him on his study, and prophetically spoke that there was an anointing on him, and God had great plans for his life. Eric was hungry to know exactly what God had planned for him, so he asked, "What are the plans?" The Pastor said, "It's not my place to tell you right now, but God will have to reveal it to you when you're ready."

Although there was something that kept drawing Eric back to this little church in the school building, there was one thing Eric hadn't done yet, and that was stay for an entire service from beginning to end, including the alter call. On one particular Sunday, the service started with praise and worship music as usual, then Prayer, Pastor's sermon, followed by altar call. Eric usually managed to get out of the service just before the altar call, however, just as the pastor invited everyone up to the altar to pray, Eric thought he'd watch this all play out and then leave. So as he sat there, someone behind him asked him if he would like to go to the altar. Being the polite guy that Eric was, and not wanting to appear rude and make the guy feel foolish, he agreed to go. Eric said that as he was walking towards the altar, something began to draw him closer. Emotion began to surge within the depths of his soul. Suddenly it felt as if weights were being taken off of his wrists and ankles. The moment he stepped foot onto the altar, the Holy Ghost washed over him. Eric doesn't remember a lot other than speaking in tongues and feeling a surge of unspeakable joy. Eric likes to call this his Damascus experience. It was an experience that would change our lives forever.

You may be wondering what an altar call is. According to Wikipedia an altar call is a practice in some evangelical churches, in which those who wish to make a new spiritual commitment to Jesus Christ are invited to come forward publicly. It is so named because the supplicants gather at the altar, located at the front of the church. In the Old Testament, an altar was where sacrifices were made. So, the name "altar call" refers to a believer "offering" themselves on an altar to God, as in Romans 12:1-2 1

It's funny sometimes how patient God is and how stubborn we can be. Eric knew that God was drawing him into something special, but this was something that he just wasn't expecting.

When Eric came home that day after being filled with the Holy Spirit, I knew that there was something different about him. I looked at him and I asked, "What is different about you?" He looked me in the eye and said, "I was filled with the Holy Spirit today, and I spoke in tongues." There seemed to be such a lightness and joy about him as he continued telling me about his experience. Although it was nice to see him so happy and full of joy, I seemed to become irritated because I knew where this was leading. He found his church and now I was going to have to leave the church that I was serving in. I must admit though, I was tired of not worshiping God as a family. A part of me thought this might wear off, and he'll come back to my church.

As the weeks went on, he was baptized in Jesus name, and decided to join this church. Of course, he told me that he wanted our family to leave the Catholic Church and make the United Pentecostal Church our home. I knew that it was coming, but in the back of my mind, I thought that he might find something wrong with it, and then change his mind again. So I told him that with Lent about to begin in the Catholic church, that I wanted to go through it, and after the forty days were over, if he still felt the same way, that I would go. Up until this time in our marriage, Eric had not always been faithful to his word, and I was afraid that this experience might fade. I did not want to go back to square one again, and after all, I also had to think about all the people that I had committed to serve in the Catholic church.

During the forty days of Lent, Eric would come home from his services with great joy, but I experienced a dying process in our church. The nursery that once was thriving with children had dwindled down to about three, and the Parish Council was losing members because they didn't see eye to eye with the new Priest. Each week, there seemed to be less and less people in the church, because of a rumor that the Diocese was merging our church with three others. I thank God for his patience with me because after the forty days, I was ready to leave, although truth be told, there was still a part of me that questioned if my husband was making the right choice to change denominations.

As the fortieth day was approaching, I let the church know that I would be stepping down from all of my obligations. I went to God and asked, "Why are you letting him take us to another church?" It was on that day, that I heard God speak to my heart, with a firm voice, "He is not taking you there, I am." That was the release I needed to hear so that my heart could rest and know that the Lord was with us, and that this was His desire.

God was fitting more pieces of this wonderful puzzle together called "my life". I was about to step into a larger piece of that puzzle, and it was going to enlighten and illuminate my understanding of who Jesus was and challenge some concepts that I thought were true, according to other teachers. I was excited for this new adventure because my husband was on fire for Jesus, and he was so attentive to us in trying to make us feel at home in this new church body. It was a breath of fresh air and a ray of hope that I could have a relationship with my husband like I did with my Savior. This was the first time that I didn't feel alone in my walk with the Lord because my husband had now truly become the spiritual leader of our family.

Chapter Thirteen

Class Begins

*"...No, those prophets were moved by the Holy Spirit,
and they spoke from God..." 2 Peter 1:21*

I remember when I first started dating my husband,
how he would shower me with gifts. Whenever I would
mention anything that I needed, he was quick to fulfill it
because of his desire to assure me of his love and
affection. When you love someone, you want to fulfill
their desires because love moves you to think of them
more than yourself. The amazing thing about love is that
when you begin to move in it, the more you give, the
more you get in return, more than you could have ever
anticipated.

The first gift I ever received from Eric were twelve,
long stem, red roses right after our first date. This was the
first time in my life that someone thought enough of me
to send me flowers. Eric didn't know it at the time, but I
loved flowers. I love everything about them: Their
texture, their variety and the various shades of colors. I
marvel at how each individual flower is different, yet

look and smell the same. I would get so excited as I waited for them to open and show off their radiant beauty. They have a way of drawing your attention. And it never fails: Everyone wants to know who gave them to you. Flowers just have a way of bringing life to any room.

Even though flowers are one of my favorite gifts, my all-time favorite gift is when I receive love letters from him. When we were dating, he would always make it a point to write me a letter each day. He would sneak off at work or during his breaks to compose his thoughts to me on paper. He would give the letter to me just before he walked me to the door to give me a good night kiss. He wanted me to read it before I went to bed, that way the last thing I thought of before I fell asleep would be how much he loved me, and I'd be assured of his care and concern for me. I cherished these letters because they made me feel and know that I was special and loved by him. Even to this day, every morning when I wake up, I go into the kitchen to fix myself a cup of hot, steaming, herbal tea, and there sits a little note that he has written before leaving for work, telling me he still loves me.

Grace Boyle penned her feelings very well when she stated, "Whenever we read a letter, we develop an image of the letter writer unavailable to us in any other way. We are transported to the writer's words, voice, and personality."[1] When we write, we express our true self in hopes of connecting with another soul so that they receive not just knowledge of a subject, but the heart of the person.

The Bible is God's way of telling us His heart for us. It is a love letter to those who seek Him, and it tells of His unfailing love for mankind. The Bible says:

"Keep on asking, and you will receive what you ask for. Keep on seeking, and you will find. Keep on knocking, and the door will be opened to you." (Matthew 7:7 NLT)

The only thing up until this point in my life that I believed to be true and faithful was the Word of God. From the moment that I had determined in my heart to read the Bible everyday, I felt a pulling and a desire to <u>know</u> God better. Just like in Matthew 7:7, I had a passion to discover how God thought and how He desired me. I wanted to know Him better so that, in turn, I would know how to please Him. He had become the love of my life, and I didn't want anyone or anything to separate me from His love.

As I mentioned in the last chapter, our family left the Catholic Church and joined the United Pentecostal Church. Their services were extremely different from what I grew up experiencing.

My Catholic background said that church services had a structure or a pattern to it. Each week the songs and the readings would change, but the Priest always led the service and knew exactly how the service was going to begin and finish. There's also a structure to the United Pentecostal Church service, but it could be very different to the services that I was used to. The difference between a traditional church service and a Pentecostal service is that any moment, the service can be interrupted by the gifts of the Spirit.

When the service started, the first thing that I seemed to notice was the church's exuberant desire to express their selves in worship. When the music started, people would clap their hands and sing with great joy, without the leading of the Pastor. There would also be times when they would lift up their hands while they sang. At any given moment, someone might run around the congregation, or there might be shouting for joy. I noticed that people would start to dance and spin before the Lord. This was the first time that I had experienced such expression of love for our Savior. Although it was contagious, I was still not sure as to whether this was how God would want me to worship Him. I am so thankful for a good Pastor who was sensitive to the Spirit and knew that there might be someone in the church who thought that perhaps this style of worship was a little radical. As he stood at the pulpit, he shared with us about his first experience in a Pentecostal church and how he thought they were all nuts. Of course the congregation laughed, which I thought was a bit concerning at first. He continued on to explain why they worshiped in the church the way that they did, and he gave Scripture to back up every action that I saw (most of them are written in Psalms 149 and 150). I had never seen this in the Word before, but as I turned to these Scriptures, there it was. Written in black and white and so clear to see that this was the way that God created us to praise and worship Him.

The next thing that I noticed was the way in which they prayed. From my traditional background, we would recite a prayer together that was written in a lectionary, and the Priest would lead us. In the Pentecostal church, the Pastor would stand at the pulpit and ask the church to pray. He would state the prayer needs and then begin to pray. Here's the difference between my traditional background, and this type of prayer: Everyone would be praying their own individual prayer needs at the same time as the pastor did ... out loud. The pastor would sense that the prayer was finished and would finish by stating "in Jesus' name"; he then turned to the congregation and stated, "and everyone says..." And of course everyone would answer, "Amen". So it's hard enough just trying to pray on your own in a crowd, but when you have 50 other people praying out loud something different ... it can be very distracting for a new person in the church.

Pastor always said measure everything against the Word of God so I wondered if this type of praying was biblical. I did some research and found that this was definitely biblical, and what a beautiful truth it is. This type of prayer, when all come into an agreement about a matter, praying their own individual prayer at the same time, is called "symphonic" prayer. In the Bible, Jesus says:

"I also tell you this: If two of you agree here on earth concerning anything you ask, my Father in heaven will do it for you." (Matthew 18:19 NLT)

In giving us this promise of answered prayer, Jesus used a musical term. Dick Mills explains this in his book, The Spirit-Filled Believer's Daily Devotional:

> In the original Greek the word translated *agree* is *sumphoneo* (soom-fo-neh'-o). It is a compound word. Sum means "with" or "together." *Phoneo* is a form of the word phone meaning "sound." So sum-phoneo means "to sound together." It is from this compound word that we get our word symphony. Imagine how symphonic prayer must sound in heaven!

Prayers of agreement are melodic.
Praying without agreement produces
disharmony and discord. Jesus is
encouraging not only the blending
of voices, but the harmonizing of
wills, hearts, souls, and minds. It is
an accomplishment to bring people
together to worship the Lord. It is an
even greater achievement to get
them to sit in silence and receive
instruction. The ultimate in church
harmony is for everyone to agree, or
harmonize in prayer and praise.
Leaders and followers can agree that
this verse is the great equalizer. New
converts, and old veteran saints can
blend. Rich and poor, educated and
uneducated, conspicuous and
inconspicuous believers can all pray
together in unity, harmony and
symphony. What a joy to know that
agreeing in prayer brings desired
results. For the sake of answered
prayer, we need to set aside personal
preferences and harmoniously blend
our prayers with others. The
symphony of sound moves heaven
to action for all of us. 2

I have to admit, I liked coming to this church, for there was so much energy and joy in the Lord. There was something different about the way that they worshipped and prayed to God that brought life to my spirit. After the second service, God kept reminding me of a scripture that I had read in the Bible that said,

"For God is Spirit, so those who worship him must worship in spirit and in truth." (John 4:24 NLT)

What I was experiencing in the United Pentecostal Church was the power of the truth, which is the Word coming alive through the Spirit. The Spirit was not only with us in mere words, but actual demonstration of its power moving around us, and if willing, through us.

Chapter 14

Learning My Instructor's Name

"Peter replied, "Each of you must repent of your sins and turn to God, and be baptized in the name of Jesus Christ for the forgiveness of your sins. Then you will receive the gift of the Holy Spirit." Acts 2:38

Let me share with you one of Eric's favorite stories. The Pastor and his wife wanted to celebrate the fact that Eric had been filled with the Holy Spirit and baptized so they invited us to lunch at a local restaurant. Being as the Pastor was married, this too was a new concept for me because this wasn't so in the Catholic Church. We went nonetheless, and I found the Pastor's wife to be a gentle and humble woman, who instantly took me under her wing and put me at ease with her conversation.

After we had placed our orders for food, the Pastor asked me about my personal relationship with Jesus, in whom he'd heard about through Eric. He was very interested in my journey with the Lord and asked if I would share my testimony. I told him my story about how my walk had begun with a simple prayer and how God revealed himself to me through reading the Bible. The Pastor asked me, "How do you know you have been saved? What evidence do you have?" I told him about the one time in prayer when I had repented and had asked Jesus into my heart, and how I had felt a love that I had never known, and in that moment, I believed that I was saved. The conversation turned back to Eric and he asked him, "What did it feel like when you were filled with the Holy Spirit and spoke in tongues?" Eric shared how it was an overwhelming feeling of joy that he couldn't really put into words. The Pastor then gave me a Scripture found in Acts 2:38 that stated: If you wanted to be saved, you must repent of your sins and be baptized in the name of Jesus for the remission of your sins, and then you would be filled with the Holy Spirit, just like my husband. At this point of this conversation, I told him I was filled with the Holy Spirit. He chuckled with a slight crack of a smile and said, "Well remember, you need to speak in tongues to know you've been filled." To which I responded, "Oh, I do that all the time." The shock on all their faces was priceless: Pastor was speechless; Eric turned and looked at me; and the Pastor's wife dropped her salad fork, along with her jaw. The Pastor remained cool, calm, and collected, but I could tell that he was caught off guard. A look of surprise filled the Pastor's face as he looked at me, asking, "And when did this happen?" I shared with him what took place, and he began to praise God that other denominations were receiving the gift of the Holy Spirit too. He was so excited that he said, "Awesome! Now you need to be baptized in the name of Jesus." For it is written in Acts 2:38:

"Each of you must repent of your sins and turn to God, and be baptized in the name of Jesus Christ the forgiveness of your sins." (Acts 2:38 NLT)

Up until now, I had never known anyone so bluntly, tell me what I should do in my spiritual walk, and so it took me by surprise. My thoughts at that time were, *I am not even sure if the infilling of the Holy Spirit is necessary for salvation and now he was telling me that I was not saved because I was not baptized in Jesus name.* I loved Jesus and I knew that he was my friend and that he was helping me in my journey to heaven. Along this journey, I have had promptings to be re-baptized because I had wanted to make a public commitment to Christ, but I never took the steps to put it in action. But now, this man that I barely knew, was telling me that I had to be baptized in order to have eternal life. My guard went up and I told him, "I need to think about it and look up the Scripture for myself." The Pastor's wife, who seemed to sense my resistance, lovingly asked me, "If you would like, I'll give you a Bible study?" I told her that I would think about it.

All I knew was that I wanted to get out of that restaurant and get home, so that I could look into the Bible for myself and discover if he was telling me the truth.

As soon as my husband and I returned home from the restaurant, I went to my trusty Bible to look up the scripture in Act 2:38. As I read it, I saw with my own eyes that it did say:

*"...and be baptized in the **name of Jesus Christ** the forgiveness of your sins." (Acts 2:38 NLT)(Emphasis Mine)*

There it was in black and white, yet my heart couldn't receive this truth. I was fighting with the traditions that I had been taught from childhood, but those words that Pastor was saying made me question if I had salvation. I needed to know the answer because I didn't want to go to hell when I died, and I really wanted to follow Jesus. I was stuck. For the first time I wanted to know for myself whether I was hearing truth or not.

Before I go any further, I would like to establish what baptism is. Baptism comes from the Greek word *baptismo:* To immerse, to bury, or completely cover.

Scriptural baptism means to be completely covered in water for remission of sins. The purpose of baptism signifies death, a burying of your old life and pardons or washes away all of your sins.

"For we died and were buried with Christ by baptism. And just as Christ was raised from the dead by the glorious power of the Father, now we also may live new lives." (Romans 6:4 NLT)

When one is baptized, it deals with the nature of our sin, and it can be viewed as a spiritual circumcision or a cutting away of our sinful flesh. (Colossians 2: 12,13). Let me state that baptism is essential for salvation.

I began to pour over the scriptures and came to Acts, chapter ten, verse 48, and it said:

*So he gave orders for them to be **baptized in the name of Jesus Christ**. Afterward Cornelius asked him to stay with them for several days. (Acts 10:48 NLT)(Emphasis Mine)*

There it was again: That believers were to be baptized in Jesus' name. I was still not satisfied because how could all other denominations not see this is in the Bible? Why would they continue to baptize in the name of the Father, Son and Holy Spirit? It never mentions those names in the book of Acts when God started his new covenant of salvation through Jesus Christ.

The next scripture I found was in Acts 19:4-5. Paul the Apostle is speaking in this verse, and he says to the people who had repented to God for their sins and were baptized by John the Baptist:

*"John's baptism called for repentance from sin. But John himself told the people to believe in the one who would come later, meaning Jesus." As soon as they heard this, they were **baptized in the name of the Lord Jesus.** (Acts 19:4-5 NLT)(Emphasis Mine)*

Again it is mentioned to be baptized in Jesus' name only.

The next scripture I found was in Acts 22:16 and this comes from Paul the Apostle. Paul is about to give his testimony about his conversion to the new birth experience. He tells the crowd to whom he is witnessing that day that God revealed himself to him. He was about to come to the city of Damascus when a very bright light from heaven suddenly shone around him. He fell to the ground and asked this Power that blinded him, "Who are you?" The voice told him that He was Jesus of Nazareth, the one you are persecuting. He asks Jesus what he should do? The Lord told him to get up and go into Damascus, and that he would be told what he should do

next. The light of the Lord was so bright that it blinded
Paul. So he had to have his companion help him into
town. To make a long story short, God sends a man to
come and pray over Paul so that he receives his eyesight
back. This man tells Paul that God has chosen him to
know His will. He tells Paul:

*What are you waiting for? Get up and be baptized. Have
your sins washed away by **calling on the name of the
Lord.**' (Acts 22:16 NLT)(Emphasis Mine)*

What is the name of the Lord? **JESUS.**

Four times I found scriptures in the book of Acts that
state that as a believer, you needed to be baptized in the
name of Jesus. Then I finally found one scripture that
did, at first glance, appear to be the same formula used in
the book of Acts. As I showed this scripture to the
Pastor, he had me read it aloud to him. I read the
following:

*"Therefore, go and make disciples of all the nations,
baptizing them in the **name** of the Father and the Son and
the Holy Spirit." (Matthew 28:19 NLT)(Emphasis Mine)*

He told me to read it again, and as I did, he stopped
me at the word "name." He said to me, "What is the
name of the Father and the Son and the Holy Spirit?" I

sat there for awhile and thought, *what is the name of the Father? God. I knew the name of the Son. His name is Jesus.* He kindly said, "There is only one name under heaven and earth whereby we must be saved and that name is Jesus (Acts 4:12)." If you look at this scripture in Matthew, it doesn't say **names,** but name. As you look at the word name, it means there is only one name, and that name is Jesus. The Father, Son, and Holy Spirit are titles, just like I could be a mother to my children, a daughter to my parents, and an aunt to my nieces, but my name would still be the same even with different titles.

Believe it or not, I still couldn't get myself to allow Pastor to baptize me. My pride was still in the way, but God was not done with me yet.

Chapter Fifteen

The Dance Troupe

*"For I am not ashamed of this Good News about Christ.
It is the power of God at work, saving everyone who
believes—the Jew first and also the Gentile."*
Romans 1:16

That Sunday at church, the Pastor showed us a video
he had found on YouTube that was going to help
illustrate his sermon. The video began with a bride that
was dressed in her wedding gown, walking down the
aisle towards the man she loves. You could tell from this
video that the bride and groom were in love. The Pastor
says to the man, "Will you take this woman to be your
lawfully wedded wife? To have and to hold, in sickness
and in health, until death due you part?" The groom
turned to his bride and said, "I do." Next, the Pastor
turns to the Bride and repeats to her the same vows he
gave to the man. The woman turns to the man and says,
"Yes, I do, *but* only if I can have one day a year where I
can do what ever I please. I want to be able to go out and
party and do whatever I want without consequence." The

man, in the video, looks at her in shock and so did the people who gathered to witness the ceremony. The video ends.

I couldn't tell you what he preached about that day, but God convicted me that I was not following His Word. So, in turn I was sinning against Him. God did not want my relationship with Him to be like the wife in the video, who would not completely surrender her heart to her husband. He wanted our relationship to be based on His terms and not mine. He wanted to be Lord and Savior over my life, but that would only come through obedience to the Word of God called the Bible.

God had proven to me through his Word that baptism was to be done in His name only and because I didn't want to submit to the Pastor, I was forfeiting my salvation. I needed to humble myself and ask God to forgive me for my pride. I needed to come under authority to the Word of God as soon as possible. I couldn't wait for the service to be over so that I could ask the Pastor to baptize me in the name of Jesus. He gave me a little smile and said, "I would love to. Let's do it next Sunday."

As my family drove home from that service, I told my husband I was going to be baptized. He looked at me, smiled and said, "I am happy for you." My youngest daughter, Kelly, who was only ten at the time said "I want to be baptized too." My husband called the Pastor and spoke with him to find out if Kelly could be baptized along with me, and he said "Sure, as long as she understands why she is being baptized in Jesus' name."

The day of the baptism was a warm, late, spring day. My new church was held in a public elementary school, and they didn't have a tub deep enough to fully submerge an adult. So they used a metal horse trough and filled it with warm water. The Pastor's wife took Kelly and I to the bathroom to put on our baptismal gowns that were made of a water-resistant material and designed like a choir robe. It had a zipper in the front and the robe covered your whole body from the neck down. I was the first one to be baptized that day, and I was a little nervous because all of the church body had come to witness.

I stepped into the horse trough, and the Pastor told me I could sit down. As I was sitting in the tub with water up to my shoulders, the Pastor told the church and me that when I was completely submerged from head to toe, "in Jesus' name", all the sins of my past would be washed away. Since Jesus died for our sins, we are buried by baptism in His name.

The Pastor said, "Water baptism is about death -- your death (death is the end of something). Water baptism is your public declaration of your death. It is a public confession of faith. I have died to my old life and my old ways. By being baptized in water, you are saying that you have died to sin, selfishness and the world's ways. Water baptism is a public burial of the old life. By asking for burial, you declare that you believe something has died. There is no need for a burial without a death.

He looked at me and said, "Are you ready to make a confession of faith to yourself and to the world?" I said "Yes". Pastor said a short prayer and then gently tipped me backwards so that I was fully submerged over every part of my body. I heard him say, "I baptize you in the name of Jesus Christ for the remission of your sins." When I came up out of the water everybody cheered and praised God. I felt different, and the best way I could describe it would be that: I felt a lightness and freedom that I had not experienced since my early childhood: A period of time when I didn't have a care in the world. It was amazing to see how so many people were happy for me: Many cheered; some cried; and others just praised the Lord. The Pastor asked me how I felt, and I just began to giggle because I felt giddy with great joy.

As I was sitting in the tub, the Pastor said, "Today you have said goodbye to your old life (self), and are now saying hello to being a new creation in Christ Jesus." A major benefit to you is the clean break that water baptism makes with your past. When the devil brings temptations and accusations, concerning your old life -- you can say "That person is dead and buried. I am a new person in Christ."

I was so excited with this new revelation that my past had been washed away by the blood of Jesus Christ. What was I going to do as a new creation in Christ? I couldn't wait to share this joy that was spilling out of me with my family. I wanted to be involved in the work of the Lord as soon as possible because a fire, or you could say a passion, was driving me forward to love others with this Good News. My focus from that moment forward was that our children would believe the Good News and receive this beautiful truth. It's the truth that: God loves us, that He hasn't left us behind to fend for ourselves but desires to live in union with us. Bringing us into the fullness of His Kingdom where we will live with Him forever.

I thank God for Youth Pastors. I believe that they may have one of the hardest ministries in the church, but that they can be the most evangelistic group when they catch fire. As anyone knows who raises a teenager, it's a crucial time of life. They have a desire to know what their values are and what they believe in. As if that's not enough, they are growing emotionally and physically too. It can be such a confusing time in their lives if they don't have a good leader in their life.

I am grateful that God brought us to a church that had

a vibrant youth group. They would meet every Wednesday night and have a Bible study along with fellowship. On Friday night, the teens would have an opportunity to invite their friends from the neighborhood or school. There were many social activities for them at the church to have fun. This young group of teens would faithfully call up our children and personally invite them to the Friday night activities. They would even go out of their way to come and pick them up, and drive them home after the event. As a parent that lived a good thirty minutes from the church, this was amazing to me: Young people who cared about our children like an older brother or sister. Again, there was something different about this church that I had never experienced before in a church body: There was genuine love for each other, as if we truly were brothers and sisters in one family. I was seeing love in action, where the older youth were giving their times and resources so the younger youth could learn how to love too.

Eric and I began to share our experiences with our children so that they could learn and understand the Good News that we had discovered through Scripture. Every Sunday, as the Pastor closed his sermon, he would invite those who wanted to come down to the altar. He would also ask if there was anyone who wanted to seek after the Holy Spirit. Each Sunday, Eric and I would begin to pray under our breath that our children would respond to the call and go down and repent of their sins. We asked God to be the Lord and Savior of their lives, knowing that He would fill them with His Holy Spirit with utterances of speaking in tongues.

The first one to respond to the call was our fifteen-year-old daughter, Courtney. She told me "I felt such a need for God's forgiveness that all I wanted to do was get to that altar, and confess my sins to the Lord." As she began to pray, tears began to stream down her face. The Pastor was sensitive to her needs, and he encouraged her to receive the love of God through the Holy Spirit. He asked her, "Do you want to be filled with the Holy Spirit?" She answered "Yes". The Pastor instructed her to praise God aloud so that she could hear herself when He filled her.

She began to lift her arms and praise Him, and within a few minutes, she began to speak in tongues, as the Spirit gave her the utterance. What celebration there was in the church when they heard that one more soul believed the Good News and was filled with the Holy Spirit.

Courtney was baptized the next week in service. We were so excited for her, and even though she did not have a great understanding of the Bible and what pleased God, she began to have a hunger for more of His presence. She began to invite her then-boyfriend to youth events, and he even offered his parents home to facilitate a

Friday night youth activity. The more she hung out with the kids from the youth group, the more we began to see a change happening in her life. It was not over night, but a gradual desire to apply what she learned through the Word of God had begun to change her so much that her friends at school began to persecute her for her beliefs. I Praise God That Courtney stood strong in her faith.

In August, Joshua was filled with the Holy Spirit at a Youth Congress in Ohio. Our Youth Pastor was standing next to him during the worship part of the service when Josh just lifted his hands and began to speak in tongues. God knows when our heart is ready to receive His Spirit. He fills you. There is no magic formula to being filled with the Spirit. It just takes a repented heart, filled with faith in the Lord to perform His Word.

Youth Congress is a nationwide gathering of all the youth in the United Pentecostal Church in America. Every two years, this conference is held and it is a great way to have the youth experience and see other kids, their own age, worshiping God together. There are so many youth that come to these conferences that they pretty much take over a city. Every where they go, they will run into other youth who have responded to the Word and who have experienced the supernatural power of God in them.

As soon as he returned from the conference, Josh was baptized in the name of Jesus for the remission of his sins, and he became a new creation in Christ. Not long after Josh was filled with the Holy Ghost, Kelly, our ten-year-old, was the last to be filled. It's amazing to watch childlike faith unleashed into the atmosphere. Little Kelly just kneeled at the altar the following Sunday.
The Pastor's daughter came and began to pray with her. It wasn't long until Kelly was filled with the Holy Ghost and speaking in other tongues.

As parents, it was such a relief and joy to know that the children God had entrusted to us were saved and would have eternal life. We all had a lot to learn about God, but at least we could rest knowing that we were secure in Christ. This is a beautiful scripture that is given to believers who are in Christ. It's found in the Book of Romans, Chapter 8, verses 38 and 39:

"And I am convinced that nothing can ever separate us from God's love. Neither death nor life, neither angels nor demons, neither our fears for today nor our worries about tomorrow—not even the powers of hell can separate us from God's love. 39 No power in the sky above or in the earth below—indeed, nothing in all creation will ever be able to separate us from the love of God that is revealed in Christ Jesus our Lord." (Romans 8:38-39 NLT)

My prayer for you is that you would be able to receive God's Word as it is written in the Bible. Don't be stubborn like me and think that you don't need to follow the Word to the full extent. That's just your flesh wanting to be right. The Bible says: God is the same yesterday, today, and forever. The formula doesn't change. Just surrender and receive the peace, knowing you are being obedient to the Word of God. Which is His will and purpose for your life.

When it's hard to change your mind remember that the Lord said in Isaiah 55:9.

"For just as the heavens are higher than the earth, so my ways are higher than your ways and my thoughts higher than your thoughts." (Isaiah 55:9 NLT)

In essence, He is saying that you might not always be right or others might not have given you the full truth because they themselves don't have it. But if you study His Word you will know the truth, and it will set you free. Free to live in peace with your God, knowing that you please Him because you believed His Word and had faith to act on it.

My final thought comes from James 2:14:

"What good is it, dear brothers and sisters, if you say you have faith but don't show it by your actions? Can

that kind of faith save anyone?" (James 2:14 NLT)

If you want to be saved, you must follow what the Word of God tells you so you can receive salvation. The gospel's three parts correspond with Christ's death, burial and resurrection. Just as Christ died on the cross through repentance, we too die to our sinful and selfish ways. In Christ, we are buried by baptism in Jesus' name and filled with the Holy Spirit. The same Spirit that brought Christ back to life. It is not enough just to believe the Word of God, for it says in James 2:19:

"You say you have faith, for you believe that there is one God. Good for you! Even the demons believe this, and they tremble in terror." (James 2:19 NLT)

Faith without works is dead. So believing is the first step, but it requires obedience.

It's up to you now. Will you act in faith to the truth that has been revealed to you through God's Word? Find a church that will baptize you in the name of Jesus and allow God to fill you with His Spirit with the evidence of speaking in tongues. God never changes and He established the New Testament covenant through His Words when He spoke them through Peter in the book of Acts 2:37,38:

"Peter's words pierced their hearts, and they said to him

and to the other apostles, 'Brothers, what should we do,'
[38] Peter replied, 'Each of you must repent of your sins and
turn to God, and be baptized in the name of Jesus Christ
for the forgiveness of your sins. Then you will receive the
gift of the Holy Spirit." (Acts 2:37-38 NLT)

Chapter Sixteen

Encore

"You love him even though you have never seen him. Though you do not see him now, you trust him; and you rejoice with a glorious, inexpressible joy." 1 Peter 1:8

Years ago before cell phones, my friend's family moved across the state from one small town to another, and it was necessary to travel through a large city on the way. The mother drove a separate car, following behind the father, who carried the only map. She worked hard to keep up, but she lost sight of him in the city's congested traffic, and the two got separated. Not accustomed to driving on streets with lines painted on them, the women found herself driving aimlessly through an unfamiliar city, looking for the right direction.

I learned a valuable lesson from that women's frightening experience: When traveling through unfamiliar territory, it is wise to follow closely behind the one who leads us. If too much distance is permitted between ourselves and the one who knows the way, we may wind up drifting off course.

Jesus is our one true source of wisdom, knowledge and understanding of God's plan for salvation. Truth is found only in the Bible. His Word has been established from the beginning of time and every promise is true. Looking back on my life now, I see that God's Spirit was always around me willing and waiting to help me in every situation I found myself in. One of my favorite promises in the Bible when I struggle is from Hebrews 13:5b:

"I will never fail you. I will never abandon you."
(Hebrews 13:5b NLT)

When I face new challenges or I need to let go of old thoughts that I thought were true, I remember this verse. He is stronger than any person here on earth, no matter how great I think they are. Further, I can always trust Him to help me because He is always faithful to His Word. The Lord can handle all your doubts and fears, but you must open up your heart and allow Him to come in and change you.

The definition of faith is found in the book of Hebrews 11:1:

"Faith is the confidence that what we hope for will actually happen; it gives us assurance about things we

cannot see." (Hebrews 11:1 NLT)

The Bible tells us without faith, it is impossible to please God. I ask you today: What is your faith for salvation in? Is it in what your parents have taught you or maybe in a trusted friend? Could it be in your own thoughts and experiences that govern Who you think God is and how He saves? The only way to know God is to read his Word, pray and accept it as truth. This Knowledge of God's Word must move from your head to your heart. Through the Holy Spirt, our God can transform you into the likeness of His Son if you just believe His Word. Only then can you experience the anointing power of God, moving through you to impact this world for His Kingdom.

Jesus is the one Who died for us so that we could be saved from our sins and receive eternal life. Without Jesus, we have chosen to reject God's Son, and the Bible says you will be judged:

"And the judgment is based on this fact: God's light came into the world, but people loved the darkness more than the light, for their actions were evil. ²⁰ All who do evil hate the light and refuse to go near it for fear their sins will be exposed. ²¹ But those who do what is right come to the light so others can see that they are doing what God wants." (John 3:19-21 NLT)

It's human nature to want to understand everything in God's Word before you believe it or stand on it as truth; but that is not how God's plan works. You must first believe and then you'll receive. It is only by faith that you can please God and receive his blessings.

"And it is impossible to please God without faith. Anyone who wants to come to him must believe that God exists and that he rewards those who sincerely seek him." (Hebrews 11:6 NLT)

You don't need to understand why God chose to put his Spirit in us with the evidence of speaking in tongues, but that is how we know we are filled. Some of my Catholic friends have a hard time accepting this truth. I ask them this question, "If Peter, the Apostles, and Mary, the mother of Jesus were filled with the Holy Spirit by speaking in tongues, why don't you think you need to be?"

*"They all met together and were constantly united in prayer, along with **Mary the mother of Jesus**, several other women, and the brothers of Jesus." (Acts 1:14 NLT) (Emphasis Mine)*

"On the day of Pentecost all the believers (this includes Peter, the apostles and the mother of Jesus) were meeting together in one place. ² Suddenly, there was a sound from heaven like the roaring of a mighty windstorm, and it

filled the house where they were sitting. ³ Then, what looked like flames or tongues of fire appeared and settled on each of them. ⁴ And everyone present was filled with the Holy Spirit and began speaking in other languages, as the Holy Spirit gave them this ability." (Acts 2:1-4 NLT) (My Insertion)

Many people teach that all you need to do in order to be saved is believe that Jesus died on the cross for them; that's true, for we need to have faith in the works of the cross for us to come to place of repentance.

"So that at the name of Jesus every knee should bow, in heaven and on earth and under the earth, 11 and every tongue confess that Jesus Christ is Lord, to the glory of God the Father." (Philippians 2:10-11 NLT)

When we recognize the power and the love of God towards us, even though we have sinned, it is only at this point we can humble ourselves and submit to the authority of Jesus Christ. After we understand that Jesus is God and He is our Father, we need to allow the Lord to have control of every area of our lives.

There was a man in Bible named Nicodemus who was a Pharisee. A Pharisee is one sect of the Jewish Priests, who emphasized keeping every detail of the Mosaic Law. Pharisees were very respected people in their society because of their knowledge of God's Word.

They believed in the supernatural and in the activity of angels. They also took great pride in their privileged status as "sons of Abraham," often boasting in their racial heritage.

One night after dark, Nicodemus snuck away to find Jesus. He had great respect for the Lord because he saw the miraculous signs and wonders he had performed and knew God must be with him. Before Nicodemus could even ask Jesus a question about the Kingdom of God, Jesus makes this statement to him:

"Jesus replied, "I tell you the truth, unless you are born again, you cannot see the Kingdom of God." (John 3:3 NLT)

Nicodemus asks Jesus how can a grown man be born again? Jesus answers him with John 3:5:

"Jesus replied, "I assure you, no one can enter the Kingdom of God without being born of water and the Spirit." (John 3:5 NLT)

If salvation came by just repenting and asking the Lord into your heart, why would Jesus tell Nicodemus that he would have to be born of the water (baptism) and born of the Spirit (infilling of the Holy Spirit)? This new concept or revelation for Nicodemus greatly troubled him. Jesus goes on to tell Nicodemus, "Because you will not trust me that I am the Son of God you are living in spiritual darkness." (John 3:18) "That you prefer to live in the darkness out of fear of your sins being exposed." (John 3:20) What are the sins Jesus is talking about that would be exposed? His sin was that he wouldn't believe Jesus, the living breathing Word of God.

When you're filled with the Holy Spirit, it will empower you to go beyond your thoughts into the supernatural realm where God is. Through the Spirit, we are connected to Jesus to be able to fulfill God's dream that He has predestined before you were ever born. He saved you by the power of the cross, and He fills you by the power of His resurrection. This resurrection power enables you to know God personally and empowers you to do the things He directs you through the Word of God. He gives us a life that is complete and whole that spills out into the world to draw others to Christ. This is the abundant life that God wants to give you through your faith in the works of Christ and the power of his Holy Spirit. The Holy Spirit allows you to experience God and gives you strength for the journey home.

"The thief's cometh not, but for to steal, and kill, and to destroy. I am come that they might have life, and that they might have it more abundantly." (John 10:10 NKJ)

This word "abundant" in the Greek is 'perisson,' meaning "exceedingly, very highly, beyond measure, more, superfluous, a quantity so abundant as to be considerably more than what one would expect or anticipate." In short, Jesus promises us a life far better than we could ever imagine.

Chapter Seventeen

Will You Dance?

"For God loved the world so much that he gave his one and only Son, so that everyone who believes in him will not perish but have eternal life." John 3:16

My hope in writing this book is twofold: My first goal was to express what an awesome God we serve as Christians. He takes our pain, brokenness, and sin and trades it for peace and joy in the Holy Spirit. With this peace, we know we are loved by God, not because of anything we have done but because of what Christ has done for us through the cross.

"For we are God's masterpiece. He has created us anew in Christ Jesus, so we can do the good things he planned for us long ago." (Ephesians 2:10 NLT)

Did you hear that? When we belong to the body of Christ, we give God authority to create for himself a masterpiece that will demonstrate His power and love towards the world through us. These are the good works He has planned for us before Satan tried to destroy us through our sin. It's God's powerful, creative work in us to know Him, so that we can reflect His love to the world in our unique Christ-like way. Out of our gratitude for this free gift of salvation, we will seek to help and serve others with kindness, love, and gentleness and not merely to please ourselves.

My desire in writing this book is to share with the world the fullness and abundance that God has for them through His Word for those who will believe. Have you ever felt like there was something more to this Christian walk than going to church on Sunday morning or helping out in some ministry? There is more. These activities or disciplines are good, and they will draw us closer to God, but God's ultimate plan was to live in us and through us, not just for our benefit but to serve Him and build up the church. (Ephesians 4:12)

If you will submit to the fullness of His Word, He will begin to transform you into the likeness of His Son and reveal His plan for your life.

"For I know the plans I have for you," says the LORD. "They are plans for good and not for disaster, to give you a future and a hope." (Jeremiah 29:11 NLT)

Let me give you an example how God wants to move

through his believers: If someone is sick in your church, God has promised that they are healed because what Christ has done for them.

*"But he was pierced for our rebellion, crushed for our sins. He was beaten so we could be whole. He was whipped so **we could be healed**." (Isaiah 53:5 NLT)(Emphasis Mine)*

The work is already done by the whipping Christ endured so that we now can be healed. I believe the problem is with us. First we have to ask ourselves do we believe in the promise of the Word? If you answered "yes", then ask yourself is healing for everyone who is sick? If you have faith to believe that God loves everyone and you know his Word is true, you will be moved to lay your hands on the sick and pray for them in Jesus' name. Healing virtue comes through the person who has faith in the Word by the power of the Holy Spirit, moving through willing vessels. We are not to seek after signs and wonders but allow God to do them through our faith because of our relationship with Him.

"And God confirmed the message by giving signs and wonders and various miracles and gifts of the Holy Spirit whenever he chose." (Hebrews 2:4 NLT)

Living by the Spirit is an exciting and always evolving revelation of the fullness and goodness of God's love for his children. When you are surrendered to His will and begin to move in faith towards the destiny he has planned for you, your hunger to know him and please him will cause you to seek more of his promises. These promise, when prayed and released in faith, will guide you and strengthen you for your journey ahead. What you will discover is Jesus becomes your everything. The reason you breathe, move, and love is all because you found life in him.

I want to leave you with my favorite story in the Bible about God's love for his children. It is found in Luke Chapter 15. Jesus tells the story of a man who has two sons. The younger son asks his father to give him his portion of the family estate as an early inheritance. Once received, the son promptly sets off on a long journey to a distant land and begins to waste his fortune on wild living. When the money runs out, a severe famine hits the country and the son finds himself in dire circumstances. He takes a job feeding pigs. He is so destitute that he even longs to eat the food assigned to the pigs.

Mary Fairchild wrote an article called 'The Prodigal Son-Bible Study summary' stating, "_the young man finally comes to his senses, remembering his father. In humility, he recognizes his foolishness, deciding to return to his father and ask for forgiveness and mercy." 1 The father who had been watching and waiting, receives his son back with open arms of compassion. He is overjoyed by the return of his lost son! Immediately the father tells his servant to quickly bring the finest robe in the house, and put it on him. He also tells the servant to give him a ring for his finger and sandals for his feet. The father turns to his servants again and asks them to prepare a giant feast in celebration.

Another writer, Jack Wellman wrote in an article, 'The Prodigal Son' "The father represents God the Father, for He gladly receives His son as part of His family. The young son returning is a good picture of what repentance is. He made a change of direction, which is the root meaning of the word repentance. He returned to the father, begging for his forgiveness and acknowledging his sin. He comes back with nothing to offer, yet the father receives him with joy and celebration. The son felt unworthy and was remorseful. The son had come to the end of himself and was in desperate need.

The father--as God the Father does--shows His love unconditionally by accepting him back into the family. In fact, the father had been watching and waiting for his son to return. When the father sees the son approaching, indicating that he had been watching for him, he runs to him and embraces him with open arms. Here the Father gives the son what he does not deserve and withholds what he actually did deserve."2

The story doesn't end there. We all know this story is illustrative of God (the father) and us (the sons). When we return home to the father, we get more than forgiveness; we get special gifts: a robe, a ring, sandals. What do these gifts represent to us?

Aneel Aranha express very clearly the special gifts we receive before entering into the house of the Lord, through her article, 'The Lost son Part I'. I quote, "In Isaiah 61:10, we see the prophet describing a "robe of righteousness" as being one of the garments of salvation. This is the robe of righteousness that is given to all of us who return to the father in repentance and are baptized in the name of Jesus (cf Romans 3:22). We also see a robe described in Revelations 6:11 that is going to be given to all the saints who enter heaven.

It's the best robe in the house, intended for us! And what happens to us when we wear it? We become like the father!!!

"And all of us, with unveiled faces, seeing the glory of the Lord as though reflected in a mirror, are being transformed into the same image from one degree of glory to another; for this comes from the Lord, the Spirit." (2 Corinthians 3:18)

In Matthew 5:48, Jesus tells us:

"But you are to be perfect, even as your Father in heaven is perfect." (Matthew 5:48 NLT)

We are all called to be perfect. But we can't be perfect by our own efforts. However, when we put on the robe of righteousness that comes through faith, we are gradually transformed into the likeness of the father.

A ring is given to us too, a ring of power and authority. What power though? In Acts 1:8, Jesus says:

"But you will receive power when the Holy Spirit comes upon you. And you will be my witnesses, telling people about me everywhere—in Jerusalem, throughout Judea, in Samaria, and to the ends of the earth." (Acts 1:8 NLT)

Remember Jesus told his disciples to wait for the Holy Spirit and they knew they were filled with it when they spoke in tongues. (Acts 2:4) What does this infilling do? In Matthew 28:18-20, Jesus says:

"Jesus came and told his disciples, "I have been given all authority in heaven and on earth. [19] Therefore, go and make disciples of all the nations baptizing them in the name of the Father and the Son and the Holy Spirit. [20] Teach these new disciples to obey all the commands I have given you. And be sure of this: I am with you always, even to the end of the age." (Matthew 28:18-20

NLT)

This is how we go about our father's business: Being witnesses to the ends of the earth and making disciples of all nations, all through the power of the Holy Spirit with the authority of Jesus.

We, too, are made sons and daughters of God when we return home. The sandals for his feet were a sign that he no longer was a servant but a son . He had security that he belonged and was loved. In the old testament days, servant never wore shoes; only the master and his family could afford shoes. It is boldly stated in first John three and one:

"See how very much our Father loves us, for he calls us his children and that is what we are!"

Paul, too, confirms that:

"For his Spirit joins with our spirit to affirm that we are God's children. [17] And since we are his children, we are his heirs. In fact, together with Christ we are heirs of God's glory. But if we are to share his glory, we must also share his suffering." (Romans 8:16-17 NLT)

We are inheritors, not only of the Kingdom of heaven but also of earth and all of God's promises.

The love doesn't end here; there is more to come: A feast where the fatted calf would be served and where singing and dancing would be in our father's home. It was the fattened calf who suffered the most in this story. In our parable, this is Jesus, the lamb of God. All sin demands sacrifice. Right through the Bible, we see that there is a sacrifice made for the remission of sins. (Leviticus 9) We, however, have Jesus, the perfect sacrifice made for all time. For any of us who want to go back home, we don't need to go looking for a goat or ram to sacrifice; Jesus has already sacrificed himself for us."3 We can simply walk through the door to our Father's house (through repentance), wearing the robe of righteousness (through baptism in Jesus name), the ring (which is the infilling of the Holy Spirit by evidence of speaking in tongues) of power and authority, and the sandals (security) of sonship.

Have you received all the blessings of the robe, ring and sandals that God is wanting to put on you since you believed in the Good News that you are forgiven through the blood of Jesus. If you have received, you can enter into the house of God, satisfied knowing you are whole and loved so extravagantly by God, that a joy so inexpressible can manifest itself through singing and dancing. You may have a peace that goes beyond your understanding to place where you are loved unconditionally and have confident assurance of eternal life.

I am a living witness of this Love God wants to pour out His goodness and grace into your life through the infilling of the Holy Sprit. It will only come to you if you believe in His promises that are written in His Word by faith. Your father is waiting there with open arms, wanting and desiring to give you His blessing of eternal life. Step into the life that Christ died to give you and watch your life be transformed!

God Bless!

Notes

Unless other wise indicated, all Scriptures are taken from Every Man's Bible New Living Translation/Tyndale/ Copright 2004 by Stephen Arterburn and Dean Merril

Chapter Four

1 Encyclopedia Britannica Company.Merriam-Webster dictionary.http://www.webster-dictionay.org/definition/Hope

Chapter Six
*1 Canfield,Jack & Hansen,Mark V.3 December, 2010.*The hugging Judge. http://www.goodreads.com/topic/show/52396-don-t-bug-me-hug-me-bumper-sticker

Chapter Eight
*1 Matthews,Robert.September,2003.*Robert Matthews:A Tale of Inspiration on 9/11.*http://urbanlegends.about.com/library/bl_robert_matthews.htm*

Chapter Ten
1 Cisneros, James, B. 2003. A Journey from Perception to Knowledge, Peace of Mind and Joy, p.55.

http://www.chosentoremember.com/book_excerpts/C3_ex *periencing_godself.htm*

Chapter Twelve
1 Wikipedia. Alter Call.
http://en.wikipedia.org/wiki/Altar_call

Chapter Thirteen
1 Boyle, Grace. 9, March 2010. Comparing the Era's" Where people Wrote Letters & When They Did Not. *http://smallhandsbigideas.com/blogging/the-lost-art-of-writing-letters/*

2 Mills, Dick. The Sound of symphonic Prayer.
http://www.cfaith.com/index.php?option=com_content& view=article&id=6868:the-sound-of-symphonic-prayer&catid=94:the-

Chapter Seventeen

1 Mary, Fairchild. The Prodigal Son-Bible Study summary. http://christianity.about.com/od/biblestorysummaries/p/prodigalson.htm

2 Jack, Wellman. The Prodigal Son: Bile Story summary, Analysis & Themes. http://www.whatchristianswanttoknow.com/the-prodigal-son-bible-story-summary-analysis-and-themes/
3 Aneel, Aranha. The Lost son Part I.

http://www.holyspiritinteractive.net/columns/aneelaranha
/parablesofjesus/lostson.asp

ABOUT THE AUTHOR

Briget is married to Rev. Eric J. Carlson and has three children, Courtney, Joshua, and Kelly. She most recently became a grandmother to Grace Paige. She serves with her husband as the Prayer Coordinators of Living Word Apostolic Church in New Berlin, Wisconsin.

Made in the USA
Charleston, SC
31 March 2014